DISRUPT
YOURSELF

—∿—

The Subversive Spiritual Practice
That Changes Everything

K A T I E   M A L A C H U K

BALBOA.PRESS
A DIVISION OF HAY HOUSE

Balboa Press books may be ordered through booksellers or by contacting:

Balboa Press
A Division of Hay House
1663 Liberty Drive
Bloomington, IN 47403
www.balboapress.com
844-682-1282

Because of the dynamic nature of the Internet, any web addresses or
links contained in this book may have changed since publication and
may no longer be valid. The views expressed in this work are solely those
of the author and do not necessarily reflect the views of the publisher,
and the publisher hereby disclaims any responsibility for them.

The author of this book does not dispense medical advice or prescribe
the use of any technique as a form of treatment for physical, emotional,
or medical problems without the advice of a physician, either directly
or indirectly. The intent of the author is only to offer information
of a general nature to help you in your quest for emotional and
spiritual well-being. In the event you use any of the information in
this book for yourself, which is your constitutional right, the author
and the publisher assume no responsibility for your actions.

Any people depicted in stock imagery provided by Getty Images are
models, and such images are being used for illustrative purposes only.
Certain stock imagery © Getty Images.

Print information available on the last page.

ISBN: 978-1-9822-7483-2 (sc)
ISBN: 978-1-9822-7484-9 (e)

Library of Congress Control Number: 2021919435

Balboa Press rev. date: 06/30/2022

Anything insightful or inspiring in this book
is a result of the stainless Buddhadharma,
gifted to me through peerless teachers.
Everything unclear and unnecessary
is a result of my cloudy confusion,
thickened by the ignorance of self.
May the latter not obscure the former for you.

Contents

Disrupt Yourself by Expanding Yourself

The better angels of our nature. It is our iconic call to spiritual arms that has been reprised often of late. We can get through this challenge, any challenge, by calling on the better angels of our nature. It is a beautiful appeal—vital even as we face countless intersecting challenges personally, socially, politically, environmentally. Recent times have laid bare that we need to do this, being human, better if we want to see a sustainable future for ourselves and generations to follow. Rather than playing to our and others' base instincts, now more than ever, we must call forth the better angels of our nature.

The question is how do we do this? We hear speeches, sermons, talks that are hopeful, inspiring, even chiding, and it tickles our American psyche of self-improvement. We feel ready, so ready, to be better. We pursue what we are taught to pursue to create a life that feels good, responsible, better not only for ourselves but also for others. Yet, the whole human situation still feels precarious, increasingly so—and we are exhausted. Pre-pandemic, a friend put it to me this way: "I did exactly what I was supposed to do. I got the job. I married the person. We had the kids. And it's not emotionally, logistically or financially sustainable. It's not sustainable in any way." Prime pandemic, another friend cut to the chase: "If I started screaming right now, I might not stop." Amidst our physical, emotional, political, even spiritual fatigue, we now have to give rise to more robust morality? Seriously, how?

With this book, I am offering a fresh take on an age-old approach to revealing the better angels of our nature that is everyday doable, potentially mighty and surprisingly subversive—ethics practice. I came upon the power of ethics practice the way we come upon the power of all practices—by being desperate.

Like many of us, I have a life story of twists and turns, all founded in the push-pull of trying to be better at life or seek relief from life. The resume version is Harvard BA, Stanford MBA and Master of Divinity from Naropa University—I'm a Buddhist chaplain, mind and life coach, yoga and meditation instructor and author who has been a corporate consultant, worked at an education startup, coached business school applicants and taught courses in business ethics and social innovation at the University of Colorado and Naropa.

Of course, those career twists and turns were influenced by mental and physical health twists and turns, which include relentless overachievement matched by ruthless self-sabotage, rounds of disordered eating and exercising, a romantic track record of trying to please men or trying to hide from them and rotating inexplicable ailments like debilitating digestive sensitivities, searing vaginal pain and a vanished period for years of prime baby-making time.

The underlying truth of the journey is that sometimes, like many of us, I haven't wanted to be alive. It hasn't felt sustainable to endure human life, let alone do it better. In the corporate years post-Stanford, my good-girl-approved method of acting out via self-destructive starvation spiraled out of control. My body was finally acquiescing to my mind's ambivalence over existence. I lay in bed at night with labored breath and chest pains and knew that the choice was upon me—would I stay or go?

Fortunately, at that time, I stumbled upon the big twist that has inspired the rest of my turns. I encountered potent spiritual technology—initially through Hatha Yoga and then my heart's path of Tantric Buddhism—that's not only kept me here but also expanded my mind around the awesome potential of living a human life. It made my life sustainable—in terms of wanting to get out of bed and wanting to discover what's possible for humanity. It has turned life into an adventure weighted toward practice, clarity, gentleness, connection, wonder, laughter, contentment and quietude. And it isn't the sexy stuff of asana and meditation that often tips the scales. Every day, I find peace and promise in ethics practice, which sounds archaic and miserable but is actually subversive and liberating.

Ethics is the real-time practice of the relationship between self and other, between ourselves and our world. No outfit or mat or class pass required. We need only our wise and confused human mind, and we can watch how ethics clears the confusion to reveal the wisdom—namely by expanding our view beyond ourselves. Through ethics practice, moment by moment, we discover shifts in how we think, speak, listen, act, work, create, partner, parent, eat, shop, vote, govern, perform, protest, play, love, make love—all of it. And transforming ourselves is how we transform our world. Through this book, we'll consider the why, what and how of creating an ethics practice that's practical and life-affirming.

Because, at its heart, this book is about creating a life that's sustainable—in terms of wanting to be alive and wanting to explore the potential of being human. As it turns out, the inspiration for the former is often the latter. This is good news for humanity, especially right now. These days, in the face of increasing epidemics, climate change, political strife, social unrest and personal anxiety, we are asking big questions around sustainability. How can we create environmental, political, economic and social structures that allow us to continue as a species? To do so will require us to call forth the better angels of our nature and grow in our potential as humans. As the stakes get higher and results come faster, we need to think beyond ourselves to how we affect the whole. However, unless we each train our mind to expand beyond surface-level self-interest, no amount of larger structural shifts will do the trick. Either we won't bother with such changes in the first place, or we'll sabotage ourselves and the system in small and large ways each day.

What's helpful is that we each have a personal warning bell indicating when we have forgotten our better angels in favor of our base instincts—and this warning bell is our habitual contraction into self-pity. At its base, human life is uncertain and vulnerable. On top of that, we all experience traumas that echo throughout our lives. And, injustice runs rampant. No matter what our circumstances or how we appear, life hurts. At its simplest, pain is a tool of learning—showing us how to treat self and other, guiding us into wisdom and compassion. However, we habitually take pain personally. Because it is happening *to me*, it is easy to instinctively prioritize our particular suffering, as if it supersedes the limitless suffering experienced by countless beings across time. Unconsciously, we light the kindling of pain into a fire of self-pity by focusing entirely on ourselves in any given moment. We cook complex situations involving countless causes and conditions in our mental cauldron of self-centered stories that all boil down to:

- I'm not getting what I want and I'm sad.
- I got what I want and now I want something different, and I'm sad.
- I don't know what I want and I'm sad.

Indeed, narrow self-interest—the attempt to manipulate external circumstances, including people, to our liking—always leads to self-pity. Either we can't get things just as we want, or, if by some miracle we do get things as we want, our wants will change or the circumstances will. And that cycle is a bummer.

Bummed out in self-interest and self-pity, we act out in small and large ways that all reduce to our being very good or our being very bad. We do everything we're supposed to do, and it's exhausting and unsatisfying…and we're still bummed. We don't do anything we're supposed to do, and it's exhausting and unsatisfying…and we're still bummed. We end up stressed out and closed off and all too ready to say eff it or burst into tears or numb out or go ice-cold—not to mention our responses when something really goes wrong. Our cycle of self-interest and self-pity is personally unsustainable and creates ripple effects that are socially unsustainable.

The good news is that there's a lot of insight hiding in this bummed-out cycle. That warning bell of contraction can become our mindfulness bell for expansion—when we're in self-absorbed, self-pitying self-interest, we know that we're playing the game too small. We can feel it. It's miserable and claustrophobic, and we know that *this* is not what we came here to do.

We can take all of that energy we spend being bummed out and instead use it to level up. It's a more interesting game. It feels better. And it helps the collective because all of the personal leveling up adds up. But what does leveling up as a human look like? And what tools do we have to do so? Again, we can notice our feelings. It feels good when our interest expands beyond the narrow confines of the self. In fact, our own pain can be a doorway into understanding that everybody hurts—and hurt people hurt people. We see beyond self-pity to the complexity of painful cycles, and this births compassion for self and other. We seek to address problematic self-interest, recognizing this as the root source of suffering within ourselves and society. We naturally fall into ethics practice. This does not mean being a performative good boy or good girl because that's still all about me and my self-image. Rather, this means considering and doing right by each other, which puts us at peace from having less residue in our interactions. We move through life more freely and break the chain of pain. We inherently know how to do this, and it feels joyful; and then we habitually shrink back into self-interest and self-pity.

Because the cycle of pain has a lot of biological and historical momentum—we're unconsciously practicing self-interest and self-pity almost all day, every day.

To break that momentum and instead actively practice expanding our minds and hearts beyond ourselves, many have turned to spirituality throughout human history. Indeed, these days, as being human feels ever more painful and precarious, we are witnessing a spirituality boom led by yoga and mindfulness and new-age-ness and generally being spiritual but not religious. It's interesting and inspiring, and it's potentially making things worse. Because unless we're conscious about how and why we employ spiritual practices, we'll bring to them the same self-interested, self-pitying mind that pervades the rest of our lives. Just as everything looks like a nail to a hammer, the self-interested, self-pitying mind sees everything, even spirituality, as being all about me. This issue is known as spiritual materialism—when we use spiritual practice to strengthen the ego's stories and demands instead of releasing them. If we look, we can see this happening within and around us.

As a yoga teacher, I have seen our culture turn this practice into a performance piece of vanity and consumerism. As an MBA, I have watched corporate types warp meditation into a way to mostly support material success and then wonder why they still suffer. As a college professor and hospital chaplain, I witness how being new age and spiritual but not religious often lacks clear practices and instead leads people into a pit of self-fascination. As a Buddhist convert, I watch myself and friends get caught up in exotic offerings and practice goals while forgetting that the whole point is to benefit beings. Moreover, as a human being, I see us all trying to be more aware, spiritual or even religious while still sounding off and posting opinions about all that is wrong with those people over there without owning our own ripple effects in the world we co-create. We take up spiritual practice to expand our minds and hearts and instead end up smug and self-righteous. We can see how spiritual materialism is a trap of self-interest that ends up causing further pain for self and other...because our self-pitying self-interest, dressed up in spirituality or not, is *always* what's causing pain for self and other.

In this time and place, we're especially ripe for spiritual materialism. With our spirituality boom, we've unlocked practices from the structure or process of religious systems and spiritual paths. Initially, being spiritual but not religious feels freeing. I can create my own spiritual path?! Something personalized that feels right for just me?! It even feels rebellious, like we're sticking it to The Man—The Religious Man. However, by creating a personalized, feels-right-for-just-me spirituality, we might be falling in line with The Man—The Capitalist Man.

Throughout history, wisdom traditions—religions and spiritual paths—have been co-opted by dominant cultural systems because systems seek homeostasis. Through spiritual practice, people awaken to a sense of subversive connection beyond the instinctive self, and the system squashes that spiritual practice into rules or behaviors that maintain the status quo. This process is both conscious and unconscious, done by ruling parties and people like you and me. Because on a systemic and personal level, the spiritual insight into self-expansion threatens our habitual, self-centered patterns, and that is scary. Even though we suffer in self-interest and self-pity, moment by moment, there is that tremendous momentum to stick with the devil we know—which sounds like "what about me."

These days, our dominant system seems to be consumer capitalism with its hallmarks of self-interest, individualism and consumption. This is the water we swim in, the birthplace of our thought and behavior patterns. So, as we feel a pull toward spiritual practice and insight, it is natural that we take an individualist, consumer approach. In a time rife with access to more and diverse spiritual teachings, our self-interested approach often looks a little something like this…

Enough with you, Big Daddy Sky God!

Then, with all of our American entitlement and newfound ethereality, we make our way to the Spiritual Buffet. And we load up—we're Americans!

Mmmmm. I'll have some yoga. Oh, just the physical practice, thanks. Who knew spirituality was going to be so good for my butt?!

I'll take some meditation. No hocus-pocus, just neuroscience and focus. Who knew spirituality was going to be so good for my bottom line?!

I'll take some Law of Attraction, so I can manifest all the stuff I want.

I'll take some mysticism—not sure what that is, but pretty sure I want some.

I'll take some tarot and astrology and incense and candles and prayer beads and Burning Man and shamanism and shrooms and…

Tantric sex?!—I'm really not sure what that is, but I'm probably gonna need more incense and candles!!

Here's what we don't do at the Spiritual Buffet…

Ooh, ethical precepts! Did you all see these ethical precepts?! These look so good! I haven't had commandments since I was a kid!!

We don't do that. Because ethics practice seems tired or obvious or not as hip as handstands, brainwaves and sun signs. I mean, who wants to hear "thou shalt not" when there's tantric sex on the table?

But, when we approach spirituality with our instinctive, self-interested, consumer mindset, we shop for practices that seem comfortable or interesting or trendy, that might help us become more successful or attractive or cool. We might be keeping calm, but we're carrying on with our habitually human and consumer capitalist agenda of "what about me." Now strategically hidden in spiritual materialism—"what about *spiritual* me." We end up using spiritual practice to practice self-interest. And, as we'll discuss, all of our micro- and macro-level problems, from anxiety and addiction to human rights violations and overconsumption of the planet, stem from getting stuck in ourselves.

So let's consider this view: The point of spiritual practice is not to further your self-interest. The point of spiritual practice is to disrupt yourself—to disrupt the momentum of habitual thought and behavior patterns that are all essentially "what about me." To that end, wisdom traditions generally start us off with self-disrupting ethics practice so we break the trance of "what about me" and say, "How you doing?"

Many of those "thou shalt not's" are simply thou shalt not forget that other people exist and their lives and feelings are just as important as yours. It's an essential but easily ignored step. When we make up our own spiritual plate instead of following a proven path, we often miss the most potent offerings because they appear uncomfortable or boring. Yet, these are often the practices that free us from painful self-interest. In fact, if we don't do these self-disrupting practices first, we use other practices to create spiritual prisons of self-absorption. Ethics practice is the practice of self-disruption in that it expands our sense of self beyond ourselves. We need not get back in bed with old time religion or abandon our yoga, meditation, shamanic journeying, tantric sex or anything. But, unless we take on ethics as an introductory or parallel practice, we're missing the point.

Moreover, ethics practice helps us reclaim the subversive intention of spiritual practice. Many of us do not realize that our personal spiritual practice and resultant behavior can help us dismantle pervasive anxiety, addiction, racism, sexism, homophobia, warmongering, environmental degradation, etc. Ethics practice is really the way to stick it to The Man because all of that habitual self-interest further drilled into us by consumer capitalism looks different when our sense of self expands to include others and the natural world. Ethics practice provides an organizing structure for accelerating our awakening into the wisdom of interdependence and its expression of compassionate action. This changes everything for us personally and then collectively.

In this book, we'll explore and create a basic ethics practice. We'll use the five ethical precepts for lay Buddhists because they are a good catchall for various ethical precepts and these are the ethics that I employ. Of course, the practice transfers to the Ten Commandments or the Yamas and Niyamas or whatever speaks to your heart. The five ethics are: not taking intoxicants, not taking what is not given, not harming living beings, not lying or using divisive or idle speech, not engaging in sexual misconduct. At a surface level, that sounds like a snooze fest. But, these ethics enable us to dig into the stuff of being human—addiction, relationships, community, planet, work, shopping, discrimination, violence, appearance, talking, listening, media, social media, sex.

We'll look at each ethic on three levels—trimming the weeds (the face value of the ethic), pulling out the roots (the shift in thinking the ethic inspires) and cultivating the seeds (how the ethic reveals the inherent insight of the human mind and heart). Each ethic gets one chapter that combines storytelling with contemplation and instruction. I use storytelling because, as the rabbis know, humans learn best through stories and this book is the product of my tried-and-true efforts with these ethics. I offer contemplation via experiments because, as the Buddha instructed, take nothing on faith but instead try practices and see how they work.

Ideally, we walk away with no-big-deal, day-to-day, moment-by-moment tools of body, speech and mind to decrease pain and isolation and increase joy and connection.

It is easy to feel defeated these days. We live in a world suffering from political division, climate change and social injustice. We inwardly struggle with fatigue, anxiety and depression. It all often feels like too much, yet we still have that spark of wanting to not only feel better but also do better. We still want to become the better angels of our nature. Ethics practice helps us answer this call—it helps us consider and connect with others, thus alleviating our loneliness and alienation; it helps us intentionally take the small steps that add up to large-scale change for humanity and the environment. We don't make a difference by separating or arguing or pontificating. We make a difference by being different. With ethics practice, we'll shift our script from the pain of self-pity to the excitement of human possibility. Ethics practice makes life sustainable in that it inspires us to live up to our highest potential for self and other. Maybe *that* is what we came here to do.

Finally, this book is a personal offering that was born from a perceived need. As a teacher and coach, I have been looking for an accessible book that welcomes our contemporary culture into awakening via ethics, the traditional starting point for wisdom traditions. Unable to find such a book, I decided to write it myself. I'm not perfect. I'm on a path. You'll see me working with ethics through the stuff of life. You'll see my pain in being human. You'll see my relapses into self-pity. And you'll see my straight up joy. An astrologer once said to me, "You are a creature of joy. But when you touch the pain of human suffering you go all the way down to the bottom." #scorpioproblems. But, perhaps, this is true for all of us. As someone whose spiritual twists and turns have led her from classrooms to boardrooms to hospital rooms, from yoga studios and Buddhist temples to pathways out of incarceration and houselessness, here is what I know for sure: We can all be creatures of joy...and we can all go all the way down to the bottom. The only way we make it through these twists and turns is by growing up with each other. This book is a small offering to the joint venture of human potential.

The Cool Boredom of Being a Grown-Up
Not Taking Intoxicants

Recently, over the course of one week, I heard the following from fellow humans: "It's just so boring" at the thought of life without weed. "I was freaked out and bored" after stopping mid-binge. "I'm scared I'd be bored" at the prospect of not being angry with everyone. "It got boring" about a marriage and resultant emotional affair. And each time I thought, "Now this is interesting."

As a meditation instructor, boredom turns me on. In many ways, meditation practice is practicing being bored. Raised as a standard suburban overachiever, Harvard BA, Stanford MBA, I was trained to *never* be bored. There's so much to do in this American life! As a well-cultivated product of our just-do-it culture, I learned to equate grown-up-ness with achievement and acquisition. Now in our forties, I look at my cohort and see a job well done. Yet, as someone whose career path leads me into people's minds, I also see that our American dream comes with painful anxiety and expressions thereof—the pot, binge, anger, affair. In fact, with the slightest reflection, we see that our beloved, relentless achievement and acquisition are not the causes of our anxiety but more expressions of it. Uh oh. It's all very understandable though. Our primal energetic response to the uncertainty of life is anxiety, that restless unease that something must be fixed or changed. Unskilled at being with this energy, we turn toward doing—we all have well-worn strategies for filling the edgy space of uncertainty. Truth is, we are a nation of anxious addicts in various forms, some we demonize and some we valorize—from drinking and smoking to exercising above and beyond, from sinking into porn to floating away on romance, from burrowing into technology to escaping into spirituality, from shying away in self-loathing to strutting about in self-fascination, from wallowing in fear to reveling in hope. The real American dream is our collective trance of habitual distractions from simply being with what is.

Perhaps there is an alternative model of adulting that deserves our attention—a growing up that emphasizes being or what was pragmatically named "cool boredom" by the Tibetan Buddhist teacher Chögyam Trungpa, the founder of Naropa University where I got a Master of Divinity. Like many of us, I began my education on being via yoga and meditation. And, like many of us, I have watched our consumer culture distort these self-forgetting practices into self-promotional projects—yoga becomes a parade of expensive pants and Instagram posts; meditation turns into a tool to fuel our compulsive productivity. For a while, I've wondered if our culture needs to cultivate being in a way that is much more boring.

Because we get what we ask for, I was recently treated to a surprise graduate seminar on cool boredom in the liminal space that followed leaving a relationship affected by substance abuse, which we'll get to in just a bit. My extended time in space highlighted that, in our ever-busy existence, there are many daily shots of space—brushing our teeth, standing on the subway platform, walking to the store, sitting at school pick up, going to the bathroom, driving home—where we can not only gain perspective on our addictive patterns but also evolve beyond them just by being a bit bored. Usually we start with meditation and then apply it to daily life. But, in this time and place, maybe we need to flip the script and start with small shots of presence that aren't susceptible to promotion and productivity. Because, in a world where we are exhausted by doing but then stuffing our minds and schedules with classes and apps and podcasts on being, where we complain that there's no solitude and stillness, where we long to hear the quiet voice guiding us along, there is tremendous spiritual growth waiting for us in the cool boredom of liminal space.

In the spirit of such spiritual growth, in this chapter, we'll look at dropping the distraction of intoxicants—the pot, binge, anger, affair, achievement. My teachers teach not using intoxicants as the first ethical precept because our troubles usually stem from there. Unable to simply be with ourselves, we turn to intoxicants. And, when we are intoxicated, we are more likely to cause harm to self and other. This cycle becomes all the more interesting when we consider that our root intoxication is our self-interested mind—we're addicted to thinking about ourselves. To work with not taking intoxicants, we'll look at the ethic in three ways. First, we'll use the ethic as a path to cultivate humility and compassion around the ways that we habitually hide. This is like trimming the weeds. Next, we'll explore the ethic as a contemplation on liminal space and how it invites us to release anxious, self-absorbed self-interest. This is like pulling the weeds out at the root. Finally, we'll expand on the ethic to reframe life as an opportunity to evolve spiritually as human beings. This is like giving water and sunshine to our inherent seeds of wisdom, compassion and joy.

Before going further, let me say that this chapter is the most storytelling-y of the chapters. It's heavy on the narrative because the only effective way to talk about intoxicants and addiction is to own one's stuff. Addiction is intimate and universal. We're all hooked in one way or another, and the healing begins when we come clean. That's when we start our spiritual journey for real. And that journey begins anew each day, each moment. So we'll begin this book with a relapse on my part—after a decade-plus of doing this work, I discovered how deep those roots of self-pity can go. Here I am again with this mind, these thoughts and that craving to not be here at all. As we recover, we pick up some tools to save ourselves.

However, no tools can help us if we miss the moment of intervention in precious liminal space.

Not Taking Intoxicants—How We Hide

I initially and accidentally became a student of liminal space when I was eighteen. I started college at Northwestern University and was miserable from the get-go. I got very sad and very skinny, using undereating and overexercising as a way to avoid my feelings. I was committing slow motion suicide, and I was good at it. Because I was good at being good at things. My mom suggested transferring schools, but that seemed like something for weirdos, not good girls. Eventually, the natural life-death-life cycle found me. I mentally broke down and dropped out of school. With no plan, I moved home to suburban Maryland, happened upon an internship with the National Organization for Women, waited tables at Rio Grande and saved enough money for an Outward Bound trip in Utah. In that liminal space, I did completely unexpected and messy things for the first time in my life and grew from broken to brave. I applied to a few schools to transfer, got into Harvard and had a beautiful second college career. Moreover, I learned that the life-death-life cycle is actually life-death-space-life. Something valuable happened when I took a break from my life and spent some time in undefined space.

I picked up my study of space in earnest during my thirties when I dove into meditation and Buddhism. From the very first breath in meditation, it was all about space—the gap at the end of the exhale, the pause between thought and action. Meditation is essentially forced liminal space. It is a moratorium on doing. As such, it is death to habitual patterns, aka our addictions. We sit. Now what? Our initial reaction is fuckity-fuck-fuck. In the sudden space, we freak out in the face of our thoughts and feelings no filter. We desperately want to run to familiar distractions—the pot, binge, anger, affair, achievement. Chögyam Trungpa called this panic "hot boredom." However, this too shall pass. With courage and discipline, we learn to hold our seat. Eventually, we find the equanimity of cool boredom. We stay present with the fluidity of experience, breathing our way through various mental and physical states. In this spacious boredom, there is room to release autopilot addictions and instead make conscious choices around our thoughts and behavior on the cushion and once we resume daily life.

Buddhists practice the little death of meditation to prepare for the big one—physical death. In the Buddhist teachings on life and death, death is a precious opportunity to make spiritual progress between lives. Of course, now we see that it isn't death per se; it's the grand scale of sudden space following death. We die. Now what? Usually, it's fuckity-fuck-fuck supersized. In the liminal space post-death and between lives, known as the bardo, we freak way out at our mental display without the grounding reference of a body. If we met the extremes of the bardo with the equanimity of cool boredom, we wouldn't be drawn back into the loop of autopilot addictions—we would spiritually evolve beyond the cyclical existence of beings consumed by craving. Because most of us are unprepared for the bardo, we crave the familiar and begin a new life with our old patterns. Once a student asked Chögyam Trungpa what reincarnates, and he replied, "Your bad habits." Even if we aren't into these teachings at the level of multiple lives, we see the parallel of how we run to familiar habits in this life all the time—going back for the pot, binge, anger, affair, achievement whenever we face uncertain space.

And what's wrong with that? Well, for starters, it's personally painful. Once we pay attention, we see that we crave the same few things every day, creating a mental and behavioral prison for ourselves. This painful craving is clear with substances like alcohol, opioids or even sugar, but we also crave things like approval, accomplishment or even arguments. Our lives are a big loop of habitual wanting, and it's exhausting to never be content. It's also pretty childish, like fussy babies needing something outside ourselves to fix our feelings. We never fully grow up and trust ourselves if we rely on coffee, media and likes to make it through the moment.

Further, it's self-absorbed. Life isn't all about me, and it isn't all about you. It's about me and you together. We affect each other deeply, becoming different versions of ourselves in response to each other. We realize this immediately by watching ourselves at work, at home, in traffic as we shift within various interpersonal systems. When we are focused on getting our fix—be it hookups or followers or even friends— other people are reduced to supporting characters in our daily addiction drama. Unconsciously propelled forward by neediness, we use each other instead of experiencing each other. Indeed, our relationships of all kinds may be the best place for us to recognize and potentially release our addictive patterns.

Though, as the life-death-space-life cycle goes, before we can find the space to make changes, we have to live life in all its habitual splendor and then let painful patterns die. As relational beings, we see our stuff through each other. It's me and you together. For the past few years of this recent life cycle, I was in a relationship with a funny, perceptive, bighearted man who, like everyone else on the planet, was dealing with addiction. Specifically, alcohol was not his friend. Because it takes two to tango, our relationship revealed my stickier mental addictions—the classic good girl takes on bad boy to indulge her combo of moral superiority and fixing people. No doubt I've been working on the unhelpful helper patterns, especially in professional settings, but romance helpfully takes you right down to rock bottom. Ultimately, this relationship took me to an abyss I didn't know was still there.

Our two-step was even trickier because while he was on the slow boat to sobriety I was on the fast track to enlightenment. The start of our relationship coincided with my starting ngöndro, an infamously massive set of purification practices in the Tibetan Buddhist tradition. Indeed, my boyfriend was the cute guy carrot who introduced me to the lineage where I received the practices. These practices clean out the basement, so to speak, bringing up our afflictive emotions and mental states. Some stuff burns off without residue, but other stuff shows itself on the way out. Still, better to air it out in awareness now than be unconsciously dragged around by it this life or next. We can be a little angry today instead of straight up hellish next year or next life. And angry I was. Angry, depressed, lethargic, confused, judgmental, controlling. As with all of us, there is a lot of junk in my karmic trunk. Between my intoxication on extreme mental states and his on alcohol, we were a potent cocktail of painful patterns.

One night, early in our living together, the man I loved kissed me on my forehead and headed off to Sprouts to get a bag of chips before an evening of college football. "Back in twenty," he said. Four hours later, I heard from an unintelligible version of him seemingly somewhere on the Boulder creek path. After a significant internal debate on whether to find him or let come what may, I headed out and used previously unknown Nancy Drew skills to track him down. Turned out my boyfriend, who had a waning dependence on alcohol with an occasional messy night, was now super high on cocaine. In this state, he morphed into a mischievous, scary-to-me iteration of his drunk, overgrown child. To my surprise, I went from exasperated, sad partner/parent to furious, screaming tyrant. I saw things in both of us that night that terrified me to my core—namely that between his self-centered, impulsive irresponsibility and my self-protective, fear-based rage, we might be capable of taking each other down entirely. Then, a few days later, we were once again a loving couple having an evening of wholesome fun watching *Fiddler on the Roof* at the Boulder Dinner Theater. Talk about fluidity of experience.

In the two years of living with him post-cocaine night,

I became a version of myself that was unrecognizable to me. In the face of fear, there is flight, fight and freeze. I chose freeze with a side of fight. Even once he took a break from drinking, my nervous system never really recovered. I was always waiting for the other shoe to drop. Indeed, my whole life froze during this time. Only recently out of my MDiv program, I was taking advantage of our cheap, shared rent to focus on writing and selling new book proposals, but nothing panned out. Everything was contracting—my spirit, my savings, my sense of possibility. Honestly, I think life was conveniently keeping me to myself. Between the ngöndro and addiction energy, I was not entirely fit for human consumption. There is a representative at Comcast who can attest to that.

Throughout our final fall, I sensed that my completion of the practices would correspond with the completion of our relationship. The timing felt right—I would reach the end of ngöndro as he reached a year without drinking. Though my preferred death pattern was an immediate scorched-earth departure, I made a conscious choice to not set fire to the structures of my life. Instead, I talked to him—wondering if he also felt that we had completed our mutual sponsorship of sorts. Though there was still plenty of anger all around, we did our best to own our personal bouquet of mindfuckery while also not letting each other fall into the projection of the other as the problem. Of all the things we'd done together in our relationship, it turned out we were best at ending it.

Even with acceptance and awareness, leaving was extremely difficult. There were logistical reasons for this. It meant leaving the coolest dog in the world—a title miraculously shared by all dogs—who had been the gracious recipient of my unused maternal energy. It also meant leaving a tumbledown country house that had become my Walden. And, money was tight. More than all of that, I almost felt too frozen to go. Our familiar hell of addictions—to substances, emotional states, people— becomes oddly comforting. My boyfriend and I seemed to be locked in a pain pact. Years before, a Tibetan Buddhist lama gave me a nickname of a particular bodhisattva who goes into hell to help other beings. In the thick of living with addiction, I ran into said lama. Saying nothing about my life, I mentioned the nickname. With that piercing lama gaze, he said, "You visit hell. You don't live there."

The psychological fortitude required to move out of our mutually created hell was unlike anything I had known. As a Buddhist chaplain, being with myself in those final weeks reminded me of sitting with those experiencing physical death. We have to summon a tremendous amount of courage to let go and head down the death canal. There in the deep winter, cross-legged on my green couch, I quietly realized that the anxiety that previously inspired a self-destructive drive to be scary skinny during difficult times wasn't actually gone. It had just found another unhealthy outlet in a relationship that was sucking the life out of me and, at times, putting me in physical danger. With tenderness, I once again touched that dire, desperate real rock bottom of all of our anxiety-based addictions be they substances or success—maybe I shouldn't be here at all. I saw that I was still committing slow motion suicide. There was still a self-pitying voice whispering that I was a waste of space. They say that some must die so others can live. Turns out that some and others are all inside us. I looked that sneaky, shady, anxious, insubstantial voice right in the eyes and said, "You're dead to me." And I shot through the death canal.

Experiment

- For the next day or so, each time you feel that life is impossible and you aren't sure about wanting to live it, place a hand on your heart and remember that countless others are feeling that same way. Send a wish for us all to release ourselves from that self-pitying pain. Do that again. And again.

- If that thought is growing into suicidal ideation, please call a suicide prevention lifeline. At the time of this publication, here's one number—800-273-8255—but they are easily searchable online.
- Call the person you thought of as you read this.
- For a day, be the person who smiles at people in the store or on the street. Know that someone you encounter needs human connection today. Know that you need it as well. Go ahead and fake it till you make it with the smile. Notice how that feels.
- Consider that you have been the exact person someone needed in a dire, desperate moment, whether you knew them personally or not, encountered them face to face or not. And you will be again. We are all needed here.
- For a day, notice your strategies to hide from your feelings and escape space. With gentleness, notice the obvious things like substance abuse, disordered eating, dysfunctional relationships, and also the quieter things like daydreaming or criticizing self and other. Know that you are not alone in this.
- If it's time—and we know when it's time—reach out for help around the addictive ways you avoid feelings and space. Know that there are countless others who have come before you and will come after you on this journey. The recovery community is full of guardian angels disguised as humans, and they specialize in non-judgment.
- For a day, consider what freedom and fun might be waiting for you on the other side of addictive thoughts and behaviors.

Not Taking Intoxicants—Awake in Space

Once we drop the distraction of intoxicants, we release into the uncertainty of space. At forty-three, I found myself untethered. No home, no relationship, no assets. Actually, that all felt fine. Yet, as I left the relationship, I got one more book proposal rejection for good measure and then saw my small coaching business dry up. I would face space with a sharp edge of career and financial uncertainty.

After ten intense days in what shall henceforth be known as the cat-pee-condo bardo, I landed in a temporary living situation with a dear friend and his housemate, both in their early thirties. The first few days were less than awesome. Sleeping on the floor in my trusty sleeping bag surrounded by shrine items and books, I missed my dog and bed and owls singing me to sleep. One of those early nights, the discomfort and sadness led to the unwelcome space of insomnia. Fuckity-fuck-fuck. Hot boredom hit hard.

Determined to do something, my mind catalogued my life as a mess: How do I have all of these degrees and skills and zero ability to monetize them? How do I give career shaktipat to everyone else and yet, like the cobbler's shoeless child, remain clueless about my own life? Why am I the queen of the three-year relationship? Am I terrible at choosing men or making it work? Am I leaving them too soon or too late? Maybe I should have had those kids that I never had the relationship or money or desire to have? Wait, is my period late—so now I'm either a) pregnant and wouldn't that be the icing on this disaster cake or b) going through early menopause and will be losing my already borderline attractiveness in 3-2-1. Maybe this is a sign to become a monastic? I'm still attached to my hair. I don't even have great hair. I wouldn't want to give up riding bikes. Can monastics ride bikes? Hair and bikes, this is what's keeping me from the full-throttle pursuit of enlightenment? Now 1:30am, the housemate with the shared bedroom wall started hotboxing me and the one downstairs prepared what sounded like a full Thanksgiving dinner. Exhausted, lying on the floor in a puddle of poor me, I wondered, "Where is the smug 'This is 43' essay about *this* situation?" Then I told self-pity that, while I appreciated her seductive display, she would not have her way with me tonight. I followed my breath to sleep.

Over the next few days, I took stock of the life-death-space-life cycle and contemplated my approach to space. I now recognized space as a chance to release what we don't want to bring into the next life. Instinctively, I did a starter model of this many years ago when I left Northwestern. Somehow that smart little girl, who had never been camping or further afield than Chicago, knew that in order to grow beyond her scared, starving shell of a self, she needed to go west young woman, put on a huge pack and walk through the woods, gleefully gobbling up every trail meal and joyfully realizing her first taste of oneness. All these years later, I knew the anxiety that had nearly erased her and lingered on to mess with adult me was what I didn't want to bring into my next chapter of life.

Thanks to meditation, I better understood that anxiety is a common reaction to the uncertainty of human life. On its face, human life is uncertain. We're here but don't know why or for how long, and we never really know what is going to happen next. Of course we're anxious. That anxiety easily inspires the desperate, disoriented sense that life is too difficult and maybe I shouldn't be here at all. Or, as one of my friends recently put it to me, "Oh, we *all* got that." And, we *all* have the opposite response that I'm the most important person alive and doing it better than those people over there. Generally speaking, our anxious hot boredom reaction to life's uncertainty is the grand project-of-me—developing habitual strategies to either prove our worthiness or affirm our unworthiness. We often run parallel tracks working self-promotion and self-destruction simultaneously—hence our relentless outward displays of achievement, acquisition and awesomeness coupled with secret, shadowy stuff around food, intoxicants, sex, internet, etc. I'm the best and I'm the worst are two sides of the same confused ego coin.

So, if I wanted to kick to the curb anxiety and its ensuing, confused projects-of-me, I needed to use this time in space to get very cool with uncertainty. How helpful then to have no home, relationship, career or income all at once. By our cultural measures of life, I basically had no life. When the student is ready, the teacher appears. And my teacher in this cycle of space was big-time boredom. After my late-night, self-defeating hot boredom hissy fit of boohoo, no job, no man, no life, I knew my habitual overachiever wanted to jump in and fix all that shit on the quick. So, instead of poor me or perfect me, I chose the cool boredom response of let it be.

To that end, I chose not to fill the space. I didn't fill the space with another man or schemes thereof. I didn't fill the space with plots of grand achievement or panicked pleas for work. I didn't fill the space with avoidance of work. I didn't fill the space with enormous practice goals. I didn't fill the space with eating too little or too much. I didn't fill the space with exercising too little or too much. I didn't fill the space with chocolate, not chocolate or debates around chocolate or not. I didn't fill the space with travel. I didn't fill the space with social activities. I didn't fill the space with media or social media. I didn't fill the space by indulging in the worries or fantasies that arose over and over. To borrow again from Chögyam Trungpa, I looked at cyclical craving the way a tiger looks at salad—meh. Essentially, I sobered up. In Buddhism, we speak of renunciation, but we could also say sobriety. Both point to recognizing the pain of patterned behavior and choosing instead to be freshly present. Rather than taking cover from the uncertainty of life in addictions, we take refuge in our capacity to be with what is.

I let myself be on pause. I still had some money to get by—aided by a few more months of cheap rent and my ability to roll with rice and beans for every meal. I created a boring schedule of sleep, practice, hiking or walking, reading, journaling and reconnecting with a few friends. Notably, there was a good amount of staring into space. Occasional coaching work floated through. Various odd jobs arose. No writing appeared. I engaged in the culturally subversive behavior of not producing or consuming much of anything. It sounds relaxing, and sometimes it was. After years of freeze and fight, I reestablished basic ground and rhythms—a process of getting used to fine. At the same time, I was working with serious career and financial uncertainty. Maybe after years of training and work toward a nontraditional career, it wasn't meant to be. Maybe I'd have to start over in some form. This wasn't a vacation. It was space. And I was constantly questioned, by well-intentioned folks, about what I was doing.

In order to progress spiritually in liminal space, we first need to respect it. We have certain ideas about what times and activities are more valuable than others—namely, moments more easily identified as doing something seem to matter more than what happens between them. The classic example from yoga teaching is watching ourselves intensely focus on asana and then sloppily toss props in a pile after class. Because what we do in the space after so-called practice doesn't count? The MBA-Women's Studies BA in me wants to quickly say that this view is rooted in the capitalist-patriarchal mentality that values masculine-doing-action-work-linearity-phallus and devalues feminine-being-receptivity-home-cycles-womb space. From this dualism, we cut and splice our days and lives—creating highlight reels of what supposedly matters, excising what doesn't. But we all know the value of liminal space. The writers know that walking and showering are the seeds from which typing grows. The parents know that the casual chat in the car was more significant than the planned big conversation. The lovers know that the fleeting glance has delivered more connection than date night. The between times are fertile. The pause is pregnant.

From this awareness, we recognize all the space and thus

spiritual potential we have in our seemingly busy lives—six months of career uncertainty, an hour of resting on the couch, thirty minutes of commuting, fifteen minutes of meditation, five minutes of standing in line, three minutes of going to the bathroom, one minute of walking to the car, the moment between thought and action. We can reframe these times as spiritual treasures—times when we can release what we don't want to bring into the next moment or day or chapter of life. Since anxiety is at the root of our painful patterns, we let ourselves get bored and be with it. We watch hot boredom arise in the form of our addictive thoughts and behaviors, the ongoing project-of-worthy-or-unworthy-me. And, instead of taking the bait and filling space, we simply notice our thoughts, feelings and environment without trying to change anything.

Though, as we know, when we attempt to release hot boredom patterns, we often become really interested in why we have the urges we have. And sometimes it helps to explore why we choose what we choose in the face of uncertainty—the pot, binge, anger, affair, achievement—especially to see the complex, constructed nature of ourselves so we cease fire on singular targets of blame, like our mothers or significant others. That said, in our individualist culture, we enjoy filling space with self-analysis. As someone drawn to masturbatory musings on my motivations, Buddhism again and again offers me this freeing realization—I'm not special. We are all pursuing various projects-of-worthy-or-unworthy-me. I run many miles, and you drink many beers. Moving on…

…to the grown-up question of how our addictive space filling affects us and subsequently those around us. Daily prayer, meditation and yoga are all wonderful, but spiritual progress demands an ongoing, real-time study in cause and effect—this leads to that. Standing in line at the grocery store, if I chew on financial worry, then I feel A, want B and say C to my child. Is this how I want to treat my child? Waiting for the meeting at work, if I fill time with social media, then I feel A, want B and think C about myself. Is this how I want to treat myself? Hanging out in the evening, if I zone out on Netflix, then I feel A, want B and say C to my partner. Is this how I want to treat my partner? What seems like a patronizing third-grade word problem is a mighty spiritual practice. It's so boring—where's the incense and flowy Stevie Nicks outfit?—but so efficacious.

Because, in our heart of hearts, we want connection and joy instead of the schlock we're dishing up with stale patterns. If we want to change the effects, we have to change the cause. Our divine mistress is that pregnant pause—she is the ultimate disruptive technology. Starting to worry, opening the app, reaching for the remote, we pause…and simply notice what is happening physically and mentally. With gentle allowance, we observe the tightness in the chest, rapid heartbeat, sinking sensation in the stomach, speedy thoughts, spacey confusion, whatever is going on. We notice without fixing—now there's an idea! When we try to fix the edgy energy by covering it with habitual distractions, it sticks around stamping its feet for attention and gaining momentum over moments, months, years and lives. Brilliantly, when we don't force fixing, the energy will shift itself. Under the warm sunshine of nonjudgmental awareness, body and mind settle down and open up. Not necessarily immediately, but we titrate our ability to be in cool boredom. Standing in line, we ground our feet on the floor and experience the sensations of being a body. Waiting for the meeting, we stare out the window and notice our thoughts flow like clouds. Forgoing the remote, we listen to our bodies and minds to find what would actually replenish us. Cultivating this friendly, accepting attitude toward ourselves translates into doing the same with all the others in our lives, from children to coworkers to partners to people we pass on the street. Spoiler alert, we all settle down and open up in warm sunshine.

Even better, there is nowhere for ego to hang its hat with these small doses of unremarkable cool boredom. In our culture of display, we won't create further confining projects-of-worthy-me by being present tooth brushers, embodied trash taker-outers, spacious line standers, quiet listeners, attentive coworkers, polite passersby. Besides, this day-to-day realization is the reason we're doing all of that prayer, meditation and yoga anyway. That said, cultivating small doses of cool boredom is a rigorous endeavor that requires ongoing discipline. Thanks to years of mind-body training, especially the recent deep dive into purification, I was able to maintain a good deal of behavioral cool boredom amidst uncertainty, which was interesting to witness considering my addictive acting out of ten, five, even two years ago around food, exercise, relationships and work. But, lord have mercy, I still faced the anxious hot boredom fantasies of poor me and perfect me over and over again. The pull of physical and mental addiction can feel like possession. We don't even remember how we ended up smoking, gossiping, checking email, dreaming of the next relationship. At retreat one year, someone asked our teacher how to do an exorcism. This being Tibetan Buddhism, there was the potential for a wild response. Our teacher said, "Lead a disciplined life."

The moment, cross-legged on my green couch, when I gave the big no to self-destruction was an essential part of my recovery, as is the moment when we fearlessly and sincerely ask for divine intervention to release us from any addiction. But we need to meet these moments with sleeves-up commitment to change. Little disciplines make a big difference. We can practice that disruptive pause all day, every day in a variety of ways. Over and over, I tested what thoughts and behaviors led to anxiety, craving, self-absorption and then tried to adjust accordingly—tiny things like not listening to the radio on the drive to a hike leads to a more aware outdoor experience leads to an absence of ruminations about career and relationships leads to being more mentally and emotionally available for a friend who needs to talk. Our Judaism professor at Naropa once joked about forepray, and I think about this often. If I want the next prayer or meditation or conversation or hike or meal or writing or orgasm or day or relationship or life to be full of presence, well what am I doing in the moments leading up to it to facilitate that state of being? Basically, if I'm scrolling away while my partner tries to tell me about his day, we are not going to be having deeply intimate sex later that night. With disciplined attention as we make the bed, water the plants and listen to others, we become the answer to our own prayers for peace, joy and connection.

Because here is the ironic good news—sad sounding discipline begets bliss. When we turn down the volume on craving, we turn up the volume on vitality. As we sober up, we see that much of what we culturally accept as normal— overindulgence around food, sex, intoxicants, media, work, shopping, fantasy—not only is neurotic but also feels terrible. We have clues of this—ex-smokers can't stand the smell of smoke, people drop sugar and get headaches from desserts, we take a break from Facebook only to return and find that it feels like a bunch of people yelling at us. The more we overlay our lives—with YouTube videos, news articles, fame seeking, mental machinations—the more we deaden our natural radiance. The spiritual move of distraction subtraction uncovers the vibrant sensations of being a body. Being still and breathing reveals itself to be a sensual and pleasurable activity. Our emotions, minus the machinations, are as well. Anger sans victim story is clearing, radiating heat. Uncertainty free of fear is pure presence. All of those feelings we stuff down, numb over and drown out actually feel pretty interesting once we let ourselves feel them. Imagine what more obviously sensual and pleasurable activities are like in this state of being. Bliss is our birthright. And it is hiding in the cool boredom of being here now at the DMV.

Experiment

- For a day, like a scientist, track how this leads to that. Notice what happens before the space-filling activity and what happens afterward. Notice the thoughts and feelings that occur right before you pick up the remote, turn on the car radio, scroll social media, take the drink, open the fridge. Notice the thoughts and feelings during the space-filling activity. Notice the thoughts and feelings afterward. Notice what words or actions follow and how they affect self and other.
- For a day, choose an activity or two to practice cool boredom—standing in line, walking, driving, brushing teeth, doing dishes. Do that activity as if you were creating a work of art. Notice mental and physical shifts and how they affect self and other. Try it for another day. Try it with another activity.
- For a day, notice the three or so thoughts that repeatedly arise to build up poor me or perfect me stories. These are our special thoughts—we give them more weight than other thoughts. They usually appear as desire or worry around appearance, achievement, money, love. When one arises, tell the mind with a gentle voice that this is only an impermanent thought. Do this again. And again. Know that everyone is haunted by the personal, demanding internal script of special thoughts.
- For a day, notice what activities ramp up those special thoughts about poor me or perfect me. Notice that there's space to make choices around this behavior.

Not Taking Intoxicants—Co-Creating Life

Whether we practice cool boredom informally through little breaks of space or formally through meditation, we see how relaxing it is to put the kibosh on poor me and perfect me for a few minutes. We're kicking the addiction to self-absorption. In so doing, we uncover a visceral, co-creative understanding of self and other. Rather than using each other, we experience each other. We sense how porous human beings are, like little antennas constantly attuning to each other. Freed from self-absorbed addictions, we become a clear channel, easily connecting with others and effortlessly tapping into their joy and pain. We see how we heal each other by being present with one another. What a gift. And we see how we harm each other by disregarding our indelible connection. What a trap. This insight into our connectedness breeds newfound respect for how we treat ourselves and others, and it underscores the need for healthy psychological and physical boundaries. It's a lifelong, fascinating challenge as an embodied human to be one within the oneness.

Similarly, we understand the connection between moments of our lives. Cause and effect become very clear. We see that our labels of life, death, space are temporal concepts we put on a free-flowing river of this leads to that. And each moment is timeless in its potential. As with personal boundaries, temporal concepts are necessary for organizing embodied human lives. This is another compelling challenge of the human experience—while we're on the magical mystery tour, we need to remember to change the oil in the car. Paradoxically, all of this mind-expanding insight makes life less mysterious though no less magical. It is obvious how our thoughts and behavior in this moment inform the next moments and chapters of our lives—and, if you're into this kind of thing, our next lives. We are creating our heavens and hells moment by moment and, in turn, contributing to others'. Life is not as uncertain as it seems. It's a glorious display that we all co-create. With how we treat ourselves and others, we can reduce our painful patterns.

These insights into co-creation birth tremendous compassion. From the bottom of our hearts, our deepest concern becomes cultivating joy and eliminating pain for ourselves and others. Childish, obsessive projects-of-me get left behind like security blankets as we develop an unassuming but all-consuming openheartedness toward ourselves and the stranger on the subway alike. We become completely invested in the whole lot of us. The notion of non-attachment sounds like it's about not loving anyone, but it's actually about loving everyone. It's about impartiality. We can actually grow to love everyone the way a mother loves her only child. For every single person on this planet, no matter who we are or what we look like or where we come from or what we've done, it's me and you together.

Compassion inspires skillful action toward the cessation of all of our confining addictions. Such action can look like any number of things—large, small, nothing at all. It can even look stern when we set those healthy boundaries because true compassion means no longer being a doormat for our own or others' harmful habits. We effortlessly fall into the ethic of discerning without judgment what creates painful craving or peaceful contentment for self and other. We consider, "Why am I doing what I'm doing? Who or what am I serving with this thought, word or deed? Who or what might I be harming? Am I fueling our anxiety with this action? Am I feeding our addictions with this post?" This is mindful living—not meditating to run faster marathons or turning yoga into a display of self-satisfied lifestyle changes or being mindful at work to increase productivity in jobs that have life-destroying ripple effects.

A few years ago, I either read or heard—forgive me, I can't remember the source—my favorite definition of enlightenment: the absence of self-pitying imagination. In my liminal space of cool boredom, when my discipline was on point, I felt a shift. I was quietly blissity-bliss-bliss, people commented on my insight over and over, compassion arose effortlessly. Then, as I neared my arbitrary deadline on figuring out work, I was possessed by anxiety and went on an extended career-worry bender like the junkie I am. During that time, I could physically feel a self-pitying curtain come down between me and the world. I recognized the sensation of self-absorption as what it normally feels like to be human. When we touch even the tiniest bit of our spiritual potential to be joyful and connected, it can be overwhelmingly beautiful. Stunned by the peacefulness of our open heart, we run back, junkies every one, to our cocoon as the worrier, drinker, smoker, seducer, binger, achiever, helper, loser and so on. We hide there in those silly, little, imaginary, melodramatic projects-of-worthy-and-unworthy-me.

Most of us want to be of help, and we are sometimes. However, we aren't much help when we're still hopped up on our habitual patterns. Because whether we're looking to score cocaine or a compliment, we childishly see everyone and everything as a tool for our needs. I have a friend visiting the United States from India. She's been watching people in Boulder ostensibly practicing something spiritual, even wanting to teach that thing. At the same time, she notices they are all smoking this or drinking that. They are sleeping with this one while seducing that one. They are buying all of this and still wanting all of that. Weary of the addiction display, she said with a sigh, "You need to be a reasonable person walking down the lane before you can bring relief to anyone." Amen, sister.

Experiment

- For a day, consider: Why am I doing what I'm doing? Who or what am I serving with this thought, word or deed? Who or what might I be harming? Am I fueling our anxiety with this action? Am I feeding our addictions with this post?
- For a day, play with an alternative narrative where the spotlight goes to those around you instead of special thoughts of poor me, perfect me. For example, your

secret agenda for any meeting is to notice what is brilliant about each of your coworkers. The line at the store is an opportunity for a secret, silent practice of wishing that each person around you be safe, at ease and joyful.

- For a day, play with an alternative life resume that focuses on the co-creative relationship between self and other. In what ways did past school or work experiences teach you about co-creating with other human beings? How might current roles be doing the same thing? Maybe learning about co-creating is always the point?

- For five minutes, take a seat and visualize the wisest, most compassionate and joyful version of yourself. See this person in front of you—what do they look like, how do they behave, what are they wearing, how do they do their job, how do they interact with friends and family. Then feel how it feels to be that person. Physically feel the feelings for a few minutes. Drop the whole thing and rest. What self-absorbed thoughts and habits are standing in the way of you becoming that person?

Me and You Together

As my months of cool boredom continued, I gently accepted the anxious moments and relished the refreshing relief that comes from being a fairly reasonable person. Gradually, without my doing much of anything, signs of life arrived. After years of asking around about teaching meditation as a volunteer, an opportunity fell into my lap with a program for individuals transitioning into stable housing. Many of them struggled with addiction and were now in temporary housing while figuring out their work lives—in other words, people just like me. After my writing mind was silent for so long, sentences started to fall into my head on hikes. After a pleasant time with my roommates, I felt penned in, like a kid ready to go to college. After letting go of plans for those book proposals, a publisher I had broken up with in a move I'd since regretted got back in touch to talk a little. And then I received the most surprising and healing sign of new life.

After my first class of the volunteer meditation gig, I got into my car and whatever talks to me said, "Go to Sprouts." I didn't need any groceries and it was out of the way, but I know to listen. As I pulled into Sprouts, I saw my ex-boyfriend's truck. Aha, the run in. I walked in as he was paying. Of course, perfect timing. Our hello was tentative—what conclusions had we drawn in the months apart. We walked out to the truck and caught up on the basics—work was good for him and still a mystery for me; he found roommates for our house and I was leaving mine for a place of my own. I broke the seal on the seeing anyone question. No, both shaking our heads, haven't even thought about it. I told him he looked great, and he told me I looked beautiful. Then, with a familiar glimmer in those bright blue eyes and that sweet Southern drawl, he said his roommates were out tonight and did I want to come back to the house. The person I felt affection for in that moment was me of four years ago because, oh girl, I see how you fell for this one. I joked that we hadn't had breakup sex and wouldn't that give me something to talk about with my therapist. Both of us laughing, I said I didn't think we should do that. But, I did want to see the dog.

So I returned to the house, which no longer felt like my house. I had an adorable reunion with the dog who no longer felt like my dog. And I spent a few hours hanging out with a man who no longer felt like my man. Our conversation wandered through our relationship. We laughed and cried and held each other and hugged the dog. He apologized for treating me poorly, and I apologized for being mean. That was that. So boring. No drinks or drama or fights or fear or sex. It was, in a word, sober. Or, as he lovingly put it, "This is so you, Malachuk. Hinting that we might hook up and we end up processing our feelings."

I told him about this piece and asked his permission to talk about our stuff with no names or details. He told me to add the cocaine detail because that was the night our relationship ended, two years before the actual ending. Then, he said, "Go be successful, Katie. That's all I've ever wanted for you." And new life dawned because in that moment I felt super successful at being human. I was fully freaking present in some of my trickiest emotional terrain. I understood so clearly why I loved this man and stayed with him for as long as I did and why I left this man and will never be with him again. Joy, pain, gratitude, anger, attraction, aversion, all of it was welcome. My mind felt vast—there was nothing too big or confusing or messy or beautiful for me to simply be with. The moment arose replete with tremendous physical sensation. Then, it dissipated and left no residue. There would be nothing to stuff down, numb over, drown out. Instead, there was so much space. And, truly, nothing but love. Eventually, we found our way to a sweet goodbye. Open and unafraid, I took the back roads under starry skies, silently appreciating the view.

Out of all of my accomplishments in this American life, it has been this recent endeavor into cool boredom that has left me feeling grown up and deeply free. Life is still uncertain, but I trust myself completely. Moreover, I value my life beyond measure. Because maybe being grown up has nothing to do with what we achieve and acquire and everything to do with our ability to be with ourselves, each other and what is. This is a maturation model of sobering up that is not taught in our culture but is incredibly life-giving.

Like most writers, I tend to circle around the same story. Telling this story—of an alternative, spiritual version of accomplishment—is the reason that I'm not a monastic. I am of this time and place. I am an American girl—born in Washington, D.C., raised in Bethesda, MD, Harvard, Stanford, Teach For America, Boston Consulting Group, even the yoga and mindfulness feel pretty American these days. I am of the land of opportunity. But, what is the opportunity? We assume it's one thing, but maybe it's something else entirely.

In the Buddhist teachings on life and death, in the same way that death is a precious opportunity for spiritual progress between lives, life is a precious opportunity for spiritual progress between deaths. We're alive. Now what? My fellow Americans, until we drop the pot-binge-anger-affair-achievement, until we release our phones and fantasies, until we stop stuffing things down and drowning things out, until we loosen our grip on all that acquisition, until we hang out in cool boredom and learn to be with ourselves and life no filter, we are missing this tremendous opportunity to bloom into the blissful, insightful and compassionate beings that we naturally are. We are missing out on not only the experience but also perhaps the whole point of being alive. And, I suppose I'll keep telling this story of our misguided sense of accomplishment and unlimited spiritual potential until I completely hear it myself. Thank you for taking this journey with me into what's possible for us all. The first step is not taking the bait of intoxicants of all kinds. Let's keep going. It's me and you together.

It's All a Perfect Offering
Not Taking What is Not Given

The other day I witnessed someone masturbating on a plane, and I lost hope in humanity. This was a big deal for me—the losing of hope in humanity. Each morning, as part of my Buddhist practice, I take a vow to continue practicing until each and every human being recognizes their inherent capacity to be wise, compassionate and joyful—initially sometimes, eventually all the time. Implicit in this vow is faith in our fundamental wisdom, compassion and joy as well as insight into our evolution as a joint effort. We can lift each other up or drag each other down, so we must never ever give up on each other. Indeed, throughout these tumultuous recent years, I have focused my mind on the awesomeness of the human spirit that continually arises within and among us as we seemingly lance our collective boil of ignorant, self-centered patterns such as violence, greed and bigotry. Over and over again, I have maintained realistic and resilient hope in humans. That is, until I saw some guy jerk off on a plane.

To be clear, this display was thrust upon me via FaceTime—the FaceTime on the phone of a woman in the row in front of me. It was the climax of a weekend where I started to wonder whether we are losing our humanness entirely. And, if so, what this means for cultivating our wise, compassionate and joyful nature—and our future existence.

I had returned to the San Francisco Bay Area for my fifteen-year business school reunion. Though a native East Coaster, I did some important growing up in the Bay Area during my twenties as a Teach For America teacher in heart-opening Oakland and a Stanford business school student in still somewhat pastoral Palo Alto. At the time, I had been enchanted not only by the dynamic community of Oakland and the collaborative creativity of Stanford but also by the slower pace than East Coast cities and the stirring light of West Coast dusk. Since then, I have held the people and place in my heart.

Of course, like all former flames who reunite at a school reunion, my beloved Bay Area and I had changed over the intervening years. For my part, I'd had a surprising, passionate affair with New York City and its relentless teamwork and vivid mirror of one's mental state, followed by a steady, solid relationship with Boulder and its precious, intertwining paths of Buddhist study and practice and solo hiking and biking. And the Bay Area, well, it took up with the tech boom and none of us have been the same since.

In our brief seventy-two hours together, the Bay Area felt unrecognizable to me. Sure, it looked mostly the same, but energetically it felt extremely different. Everyone was facedown in phones, giving the place a distracted, jittery, lonely vibe. The environment seemed increasingly paved over or overly manicured, giving it a uniform, sterile, dead atmosphere. It felt rootless—like it was running on air and anxiety, the way our bodies and minds feel after too much screen time. I talked with friends about this—natives of the Bay Area, transplants from NYC—and they, too, bemoaned the scene.

In this one-industry town, they told tales of everyone being caught up in the magic and potential of technology—how it can make us productive and efficient and happy, how we can outsource or eliminate all the boring and worthless activities we talked about in the previous chapter like making your kid's lunch or waiting in line or walking. "To free up our time for what?" we joked, "Deep thoughts? Soulful sex? Mantra recitation?" No. Mostly, we agreed, all of that supposed free time went to scrolling social media or watching YouTube, Netflix, porn. Tech giveth time and tech taketh away. And it feels sad, like we're trying to outsource or eliminate basic human stuff like connection, caregiving, love, sex. And we know it feels sad. "Oh you aren't feeling so great? Maybe you should spend more time alone and online?" said no one ever.

With this rolling around in my mind and heart, I boarded my return flight to Denver and watched everyone pull down all the window shades. No one wants to see the Rocky Mountains from above? Then all the seatback screens went on, and most folks topped that off with a computer and/or phone. All the humans went bye-bye into small, private, virtual worlds, checked out from the immediate world around us. Staring straight ahead to settle into cool boredom, I could see between the seats to the average-sized, enormous phone of the woman in front of me, which showed a shirtless guy on FaceTime. As a chaplain—who clearly doesn't get out much—my first thought was that she was talking to someone who just had surgery, and then the shot panned down to a close-up that once seen could not be unseen. Beyond the jarring effect of penis without warning, I felt alarmed. The plane suddenly seemed like a preview of our impending dystopia—living in stale-air, blue-light coffins where everyone disregards each other and themselves and feeds off fantasies on the screen. Leaving the land of so-called innovation in this zoned-out situation, I questioned whether this is the future we all actually want. And, if so, we can probably kiss goodbye humanity and the opportunity to awaken to wisdom, compassion and joy in this form of consciousness.

In the spirit of resistance, in this chapter, we'll celebrate the magic and potential of being human among humans on this planet—and how our future relies on our decreasing consumption and increasing connection. To do so, we'll look at the ethic of not taking what is not given in three ways. First, we'll use the ethic as a path to clean up our behavior around taking, which leads to greater ease with self and other. This is like trimming the weeds. Next, we'll explore the ethic as a contemplation on interdependence and the reality of our interrelationship with each other and our world. This is like pulling the weeds out at the root. Finally, we'll expand on the ethic to develop a proactive mindset of offering. This is like giving water and sunshine to our inherent seeds of wisdom, compassion and especially joy.

Before going further, I want to say that technology is not the problem per se. When discussing my tech weary and wary ideas for this chapter with one of my older brothers, he said I might be unintentionally plagiarizing the Unabomber's manifesto. Point taken. The problem is how technology—specifically the internet and social media—caters to our confused, habitual thinking that taking in more will solve the problem, which is already exacerbated by consumer capitalist mind training. Whether it's information, knowledge, sex, shopping, likes or attention, we use technology like an IV of input. It's a form of passive intake that has proven to be disappointing and ironically disconnecting. It's also emblematic of our identifying as consumers rather than humans. We take and take and take…and it never really satisfies. Because being human is about more than taking.

Being human is a relational and communal experience with give and take, generosity and reciprocity. By not taking what is not given, we disrupt the momentum of dehumanizing consumption and reclaim our humanity by examining our role in the basic cycle of survival—giving and taking. In fact, unless we each work with our human mind, we'll continue creating technological tools and using them in ways that make our problems worse. It's not a new suggestion to say that we need to develop our wisdom, compassion and joy at a more vigorous rate than we develop technology so we don't destroy ourselves. Sitting on that airplane, I wondered if our self-destruction wouldn't come from high-tech weaponry but rather the erosion of our minds, hearts and humanity through constant, distracting, infantilizing, insidious, isolating, numbing, self-absorbed consumption.

Not Taking What is Not Given—Don't Steal

For the past few years, I have spent a month each summer on retreat with my Buddhist lineage. And, each year, I overpack like a champ. Why? Because I get super anxious before I go. Retreat can be intense—practice all day, every day, you and all of your mental, emotional, physical stuff. So I bring a bunch of material stuff—namely clothes—like a defensive shield. What's particularly odd is that I don't own a lot of clothes, so I'm basically packing all of my clothes into my big backpacking pack as if I'm never returning. I know it's bizarre. I know it's an expression of anxiety. I still do it each year.

As we discussed in the previous chapter, being a human being is an uncertain and therefore anxiety-provoking situation. A knee-jerk survival response is to armor ourselves with stuff. We don't need to look far in our culture to see that we love to surround ourselves with stuff. We can watch ourselves do this in little ways all the time. As a yoga teacher, I always felt tenderness for new students who would bring towels, water bottles, phones, journals, sweatshirts, whatever. Building a little nest around their mat made them feel less exposed in this new activity. I get it. I bring all my clothes to retreat. We can also watch ourselves do this in big ways all the time. I have yet to meet anyone at any income bracket who doesn't worry about money and believe they would feel better if they had more of it. Out of a survivalist assumption of safety in stuff, we have a propensity to want and a desire to take. Our consumer capitalist culture takes this ball and runs with it by training our minds to equate our very personhood with our money and stuff. It ramps up unexamined survival mind to create our constant mantra of more, more, more.

Untrammeled, this leads us to take whatever we can get, sometimes in violent ways. This is not new human behavior. So, throughout time, wisdom traditions have offered us the ethic of not taking what is not given—i.e., don't steal. It is important to spend time with this ethic on that basic level, which means taking a step back to contemplate the ways in which we do steal. And it feels impossible to elucidate ways in which we each personally might steal when we have an entire country and dominant white culture built on theft—theft of land, bodies, labor and culture of Indigenous peoples, Black people and people of color, theft of bodies and labor of women and children, theft of natural resources...all of this theft of all that is precious for capitalist-patriarchal profit. It all continues in obvious and obscured ways. Where do we even start?

The only thing we can control is our personal actions, and our personal actions have collective results. So we can start by looking at ways we take what is not given throughout our daily lives. In what ways might I be stealing from others in how I live? This involves a personal inventory across a variety of areas—money, time, physical freedom, dignity, peace, space. It involves research and thought and effort. It involves contemplating history and privilege—how what certain parties have or don't have is rooted in power and exploitation, which will be named more in the following chapter on non-harming. In so many ways, what so many of us take has not at all been given. There are violent consequences—immediate and distant—to how we live and work, what we buy and do. Broadly speaking, there's a lot of rape in our world.

This can be overwhelming when we actually consider it. I'm giving it a broad brush here not because it is unimportant but because it is so large and personal—the changes we each need to make are rooted in where we come from, what body we're inhabiting and how we live. It's also mind-boggling to think through all of our consequences and ripple effects. But we are smart and have good instincts that let us know, moment by moment, when we're even slightly stealing from someone in some way by doing this or that. If we check in, we can feel when our actions feel off.

One old-school tool of discernment around stealing that has proven useful to me and my students in business ethics at the University of Colorado is Kant's categorical imperative—would it be cool if everyone did this thing I'm about to do? It's a gut check on acting from ethical teamwork instead of individual desire—even if it seems like I'm not taking what is not given right now, would I want to live in a world where everybody took this action? I was brushing up on such ethical tools to teach that course when my boyfriend-at-the-time and I flew to Houston for a wedding. We had boarded the plane and were about to take off when it was announced that we had a gate change—so deplane and go directly to the new gate. Once we all left the plane and headed to the other gate, my boyfriend went in a different direction. I asked where he was going, and he said that this process would take forever so he was getting a cookie. I was annoyed and wasn't sure why. Then I realized it was Kant's categorical imperative—if everyone left to get a cookie, the reboarding process would take way more time. If it wasn't cool for everyone to get a cookie, then it wasn't cool for anyone to get a cookie. With this action, it felt like he was taking time or something away from the rest of us. When he returned, we had a little argument about it. In retrospect, I want to apologize to my fellow travelers because overhearing some arrogant-know-it-all girlfriend invoke Kant in a fight with her generous-cookie-offering boyfriend might be worse than witnessing someone masturbating pre-flight on FaceTime. Also, there may have been flaws in my argument because, like an MBA, I prioritized efficiency for all over cookies for all. And, clearly, the fight was not about the cookie. But, as for the categorical imperative, we get the point.

Another tool that led to aha's for me as a college student and for the college students I've taught is John Rawls's veil of ignorance. The basic gist is what kind of systems—economic, government, social, food, shelter, accessibility—would we set up if we didn't know who we would be in the system. If we were behind the veil of ignorance, we wouldn't know our nationality, race, ethnicity, sex, size, age, gender, socioeconomic status, physical and mental abilities, sexual orientation and so on. From that place of not knowing our personal role—because let's face it, we don't get choices at birth—how would we construct our world? Seeing the expressions on my college students' faces in response to that question reminded me of my own reaction in college when I heard that question—wow, we are totally missing the mark.

Generally speaking, such ethical tools—the categorical imperative, the veil of ignorance, not taking what is not given—are an affront to specialness. They disrupt the self that thinks, "I deserve this more than everyone else." In this time and place, they disrupt the self that is trained in self-centered consumption. We use them not to be good boys and girls, which is a trap of self-absorbed pride in and of itself. We use these tools to trim the weeds of selfishness in our minds. Because even when it seems like we're not stealing from anyone with this itty-bitty selfish action, we're still creating a mind that prioritizes self over other—from which myriad, painful internal and external ripple effects flow.

To use such tools as a practice, we start running our thoughts and behaviors through them like a filter. For a morning—as we eat, work, shop, love, talk, listen, exercise, drive, walk, scroll, post, watch, all of it—we commit to thinking, "In doing what I am doing, am I taking what is not being given in some way? Would I want to live in a world where everyone thought, said or did this? Am I participating in systems or endeavors that I'd create or support if I played a different role in them?" Then we try it again for another morning. Then we try it for a day. Then another day. This is how we cut back on self-centered thinking. We simply ask ourselves such questions and see what arises from our inherently wise minds and compassionate hearts. Our speech and actions follow from there.

Interestingly, in working with this ethic, we do an about-face on thinking that happiness comes from prioritizing self over other. Instead, we witness an ease of being that arises from considering how our thoughts and actions affect others and our world. In our heart of hearts, we want to live in harmony with each other. We know that our relationships affect our quality of life. As we trim the weeds of selfishness, we feel more comfortable with our existence. Our actions create less residue. We don't need to spend time rationalizing self-centered behavior that violates our hearts. We don't need to numb via various addictions to shut up our sadness over our lifestyle.

After business school, I was fortunate to land a corporate consulting job that admittedly was mostly appealing to me for two reasons—it was in NYC where my boyfriend-at-that-time was moving and it covered my massive monthly student loan payment. However, I quickly discovered that every aspect of that job felt antithetical to my being, from the clothes required to the content of the work. Of greatest discomfort was the feeling that my mind and body were being used in service of systems that were taking what is not given and violating people near and far. I watched myself attempt to drown out my inner conflict in a variety of ways—my usual go-tos of restrictive eating and overexercising along with overly focusing on my partner's life to avoid my own life, now topped with extra shopping and social drinking, and sometimes thinking about jumping in front of the subway. Once again, self-pity almost got the best of me. It was serious. I was anxious and angry and lost. I developed digestion issues and stopped getting my period. I was struggling on many levels. Like all of us, I have a wise mind and compassionate heart. When I violate them with narrow self-interest, I feel depressed and act out. Over the years, I have watched countless emotional and physical issues clear up as I align my life with my mind and heart's inherent insight into connection.

As discussed, there is wisdom in our confusion. So now we see another reason why we turn to intoxicants rather than hanging out in cool boredom. We don't want to spend quiet time with our minds and hearts because we are living out of alignment with them. This contributes to our anxiety and dis-ease, and we find ourselves covering our internal conflicts with addictive consumption. As we trim the weeds of self-centered thoughts, words and actions, we feel better. Not because we're being goody-goodies but because we're being wise. We're acting in alignment with our instincts as humans. We want to do right by each other, and, when we do, we move through the world with greater ease.

<u>Experiment</u>

- Choose an area of life—e.g., eating, shopping, work, love, nature, internet, sex, commuting, friendship. For one day, before taking action in this area, contemplate the action through a few thought filters:
  o In doing what I am doing, am I taking what is not being given in some way?
  o Would I want to live in a world where everyone thought, said or did this?
  o Am I participating in systems or endeavors that I'd create or support if I played a different role in them?
- Notice any desire to act differently. Try different actions. Notice changes in behaviors, thoughts, emotional and mental states.
- Try it for another day. And another. Try it with another area of life. And another.

Not Taking What is Not Given—Interdependence

Here's the thing about bringing all of my clothes to retreat—I don't even have the right clothes. As mentioned, I've had a few lean financial years. Most of what I own I bought a decade ago, and it's fine for day-to-day Boulder. However, I practice in a traditional Tibetan Buddhist lineage. This means people get dressed up for ceremonies and teachings, and I always feel a little schleppy. Last year, my retreat girlfriends realized that I wasn't psyched about the schleppiness; I just didn't have the means to take it up a notch. We all know what happened next—my sangha sisters dressed me. They loaned me beautiful clothes for ceremonies and teachings. They even gave me clothes for keeps. It was both touching and instructive to be cared for by these women I only see once a year in this one context.

Because this is what humans do—we take care of each other. We have babies and we raise them. Our parents get old and we care for them. We create communities and we look out for each other. We develop skills and we share them. We engage in give and take. We create a web of generosity and reciprocity.

At least we used to. With our cultural and capitalist emphasis on individualism, which we unhelpfully export, we are behaving in a confused and inhuman way. A few years ago, maybe more, there was some political something happening that led to a bunch of people saying, "I did it myself!" They were talking about their careers or fortunes or who even cares. It was an American thing to say—I did it myself! It's also an ignorant thing to say. No one has ever done anything by themselves. It's impossible. For starters, each of us is here thanks to at least two people, most especially the ones who donated their bodies to the generous task of gestating us before birthing us into being through either a) tearing open their tender, precious, magical vagina or b) being cut open into the core of their being. Didn't do that yourself! Then countless people have done the generous work of feeding us, clothing us, protecting us, wiping our bottoms, teaching us how to move and eat and function and read and write and learn and work and so on until we grow ill or old and other people will feed us, clothe us, protect us, wipe our bottoms and help us die. And that's just the immediate stuff. People build our homes, design our cities, create our schools, grow our food, treat our wastewater, make our clothes, maintain our roads, everything. Everything! Every moment of our lives is brought to us thanks to others. We exist and survive because of each other. It's called interdependence and it's reality.

In Buddhism, ignorance is defined as not understanding interdependence. Wisdom is defined as understanding interdependence. "I did it myself" is the height of ignorance. In our culture of hyperindividualism, we train our minds in ignorance. We actually believe we do things ourselves; this leads us to self-cherish, self-absorb, self-promote. All of this focus on self leads to all manner of social and environmental destruction. We prioritize our unexamined, ignorant, me-first needs without pausing to contemplate the consequences for other humans and our habitat. We get seduced by the capitalist incentive to isolate into higher-profit personal consumption instead of sharing in lower-cost communal experience. We fall prey to incorrect survival thinking that closing off from community and hoarding stuff and money will keep us safe when history has proven just the opposite. Human beings have never done it alone. When we forget the reality of needing each other and our habitat, we take these things for granted and we lose them—as we can see now with the erosion of our communities and degradation of our environment.

Ignorant individualism taken to the extreme will have us all either extinct or living in solo boxes breathing fake air while consuming virtual reality all day, every day. We can see ourselves taking steps there and it does not feel good. The more we isolate and detach from each other, the less we know and trust each other, and the more frightened and dangerous we all get. The more we impersonally shop and outsource our own caretaking, the more disconnected and dissatisfied we feel with how we live and eat and love. As a coach and chaplain who hears people's innermost longings, I can tell you this—we are all lonely and getting lonelier. Our current trajectory feels off because it's out of touch with how humans actually survive and thrive—together.

To pull out the weeds of ignorant, self-absorbed consumption at the root, we contemplate interdependence and act accordingly. We disrupt the self by expanding the self to understand that we make up each other's lives. We see that taking what is not given feels terrible because it is out of alignment with the web of existence. When I take what is not given from you, I ultimately take from myself. Our fates are intertwined. I might not feel the effects of my actions immediately because of the distance between us, but I will feel the effects eventually in the world I am creating. What we put into the web is what we get out of the web. We actively create our world, moment by moment.

I first started contemplating interdependence when I was living in New York City. After leaving the corporate gigs, I was teaching yoga and starting to study Buddhism. The subway became my favorite classroom. I already loved the subway for gifting me examples of human kindness—the time I fainted exiting the train and a woman caught my tumbling body, forgave me for inadvertently going to second base on her and sat with me until I could do vertical; the time I saw a tourist family recovering from having their four-year-old swept into a train alone at Times Square only to be noticed as suspiciously solo by a college student who took him by the hand, alerted authorities and chaperoned him back to Times Square and his family. Now I sat on the subway and considered human kindness on a less obvious level, the basic human kindness of helping each other exist. I sat and considered how each person in front of me came to be—all of the people who raised this person, all of the people who raised the people who raised this person, all of the people who created the clothes, food and education of this person, all of the people who created the clothes, food and education of the people who created the clothes, food and education of this person. I sat and considered all of the people who designed and operated the subway—all of the people who raised those people, all of the people who created the clothes, food and education of those people and so on. Of course, I sat and considered all of the people involved in my existence as well—all of the people who raised me, all of the people who raised them, all of the people who created my clothes, food and education, all of the people who provided for them. I sat and considered the intersection of me and these people on the subway—how we affected each other just by the way we were with each other on this train, how we would take this experience into the rest of the day in some way, how we were linked by simply sharing this subway ride.

When we contemplate our interdependence with humanity, we disrupt the self by expanding it to include each other. And, when we do this, a few things happen as we make our way through the world. First, we take a break from thinking about how to get what we want and keep what we have, and that alone is relaxing. Next, we recognize the reality that other people are people unto themselves and not props in our plan or adversaries in our quest for accumulation, and that too feels like a pressure release. Also, we understand our immediate and constant connection with others, and that helps us feel less alone and more responsible. Finally, we start to blow our minds. We don't need outside substances to have transcendent experiences. We can each get mystical with our inherently wise human mind—on the subway, at the movies, in a restaurant. All we need to do is use it.

Predictably, my contemplation on interdependence expanded to include the natural world when I moved to Boulder and started spending awesome amounts of time outdoors. Initially, all of those hours on foot and bicycle in the woods, on mountain peaks, alongside creeks and among farmlands helped thirty-seven-year-old me grok kindergarten insights into interdependence—we breathe because of trees, we drink because of precipitation, we eat because of soil. Beyond those basics, as I wandered our local trails again and again, I came to know this land like my body, experiencing its yearly changes in concert with my own cycles. These mountains and mesas have held space for all of my outer and inner journeys. I don't just live in this place—I am of this place. My sense of self includes my beloved belly tree three-quarters of the way up my favorite trail, the witchy wide-armed cottonwood behind my old tumbledown house, the rising and falling creek rushing outside my current place, the hawks who teach me to pull back the camera, the snakes who remind me to be a wild woman, the mountain lions who stop my thoughts, the big blue sky that shows me my mind. Considering how my actions affect the well-being of this place feels no different than considering how my actions affect my own well-being.

When we contemplate our interdependence with nature, we disrupt the self by expanding it to include our planet. Scientifically and spiritually, we already understand this. As a coach and chaplain, I hear over and over again that people feel at one, at peace, with God, less alone, at home, in communion, awake, open and alive when in nature. As embodied human beings, we resonate with this planet. This is our habitat—we are made of this place and belong in this place. We love it, and we're grateful for it. However, in our often anxious and uncertain state of mind, our sense of self shrinks to me, me, me, and we go into gobble-up mode. All of that consumption takes a toll on our shared home. The more we pay attention to and respect the power of sun, moon, sky, trees, dirt, rain, snow, water and wind, the more we relax into the inspiring and challenging reality of being one with this place. We feel at home, we grow up and we make different choices. Rather than rapidly consume our world, we want to honor and nourish it as we would our own bodies. We seek to not destroy our world because we are our world.

As we contemplate our interdependence with each other

and our world, we start to shift our minds. We pull out the weeds of hyperindividualism and rampant consumerism at the root. We pull out that anxious, isolating, ignorant focus on taking and getting more. We naturally start to consider the whole instead of me. We lose interest in taking what is not given because competition stops making sense. We root out the weeds of me-versus-you because we understand that it is all us.

We realize that the ethical precept of not taking what is not given was developed with the insight into interdependence. We know that humans survive and societies thrive if we work together. We know that you and I and our planet are not separate. Instinctively, we know this. To mentally accept and act from this insight, we continually disrupt ourselves by expanding ourselves to include each other and our world. Then our knee-jerk, defensive, momentary, me-based preferences lose steam. We know that it feels bad to act from an ignorant, small, separate self. We know that it feels good to act from an integrated, whole, interdependent self. Interestingly, tuning into reality feels much better than checking out.

Experiment

- Contemplate interdependence with humanity:
  - Consider people who have contributed to your existence and personality. Take a few minutes and consider the people who raised you and all that entailed—your caregivers who changed you, fed you, kept you warm and safe, your teachers and mentors who helped you learn and grow and discover interests and talents, your friends and partners who loved you and challenged you and made you laugh and showed you who you are. Think about it until you feel a sense of connection in your body and heart. Hang out in that experience until it dissipates. Notice any

changes in your thinking and behavior as you move through the rest of your day.

o   Consider people who have contributed to your thinking. Take a few minutes and consider influential books you've read and the many people involved in creating them, influential movies you've seen and the many people involved in creating them, influential classes you've taken and the many people involved in creating them from teachers to classmates to custodial staff, influential philosophy and spirituality you've studied and the many people involved in creating and disseminating them. Think about it until you feel a sense of connection in your body and heart. Hang out in that experience until it dissipates. Notice any changes in your thinking and behavior as you move through the rest of your day.

o   Consider people who have helped meet your material needs. Take a few minutes and consider all of the people involved in creating the shirt you're wearing from the designers and marketers to the individuals whose hands in some form did the dyeing and cutting and sewing and packaging and shipping to the people working in the distribution centers and the stores. Consider all of the people involved in creating your breakfast from the people tending and harvesting crops to the people working in the packaging and distribution centers to the people working in the grocery store. Consider all of the people involved in building your living space from the people who inhabited and established the area to the architects and designers of your place to the original construction crew and any ongoing maintenance crews, including family and neighbors. Think about it until you feel a sense of connection in your body and heart. Hang out in that experience until it dissipates. Notice any changes in your thinking and behavior as you move through the rest of your day.

- Contemplate interdependence with nature:
  - ○ Consider the elements involved in your breathing. Take a few minutes and look at a tree and consider how it absorbs carbon dioxide and releases oxygen and then consider how you absorb oxygen and release carbon dioxide. Consider how you and the tree are a perfect match that way. Consider the seed of the tree and years of sun, air, soil, precipitation and unimaginable factors that went into creating its DNA that all together grew that seed into a tree that gifts your ability to breathe. Think about it until you feel a sense of connection in your body and heart. Hang out in that experience until it dissipates. Notice any changes in your thinking and behavior as you move through the rest of your day.
  - ○ Consider the elements involved in your eating. Take a few minutes and look at your meal. Consider the seeds, created by a previous generation of plants, and the soil that surrounded the seeds as well as the cycles of sun, care and watering to nurture the seeds into food. Consider any animals involved, from the seeds, soil, sun, rain that grew their food to the labor and life they gave. Think about it until you feel a sense of connection in your body and heart. Hang out in that experience until it dissipates. Notice any changes in your thinking and behavior as you move through the rest of your day.

o   Consider the elements involved in your peace of mind. Take a few minutes and look at where you live in the world, be it urban or suburban or rural or moving between it all. Feel the air on your skin and your feet on the ground, hear the sound of wind in the trees or birds in the sky or even water flowing past, see the sky and clouds and sun and moon and leaves and grasses and flowers, smell the air and plants and maybe even rain. Feel how your sensory experience fills you up. Think about it until you feel a sense of connection in your body and heart. Hang out in that experience until it dissipates. Notice any changes in your thinking and behavior as you move through the rest of your day.

Not Taking What is Not Given—Offering Mind

To be totally honest, my lack of dressing up at retreat wasn't only a factor of finances. I didn't really understand the point. It's eight million degrees with four hundred percent humidity, we're living in tents, everything is sweaty and nothing dries, the last thing I want to do is put on anything fancy or close fitting or god forbid itchy. I compound the comfort argument with clunky feminist thinking around not making myself pretty to please men, which then becomes not making myself pretty ever because do we even know what pretty might be after an unceasing history of prettiness as defined by the male gaze. So I end up overthinking, self-righteous and insecure in some sticky rabbit hole of distorted resistance to who knows what when good grief, woman, maybe just toss on a freaking skirt for an hour. Until one day when a friend who always looks beautiful unto herself for ceremonies revealed an inner monologue that matched mine but then countered with how dressing up is making oneself an offering to the Buddhas. And I was sold.

Offering mind is a magical thing. Honestly, it blows mindfulness mind out of the water. There's something about mindfulness as it takes root in our culture that becomes overly serious—we slowly and somberly chew our single raisin. It even becomes competitive—I am the most focused and earnest single raisin eater ever. Sometimes when immersed in the mindfulness scene, people seem sad or dull or washed out. Mindfulness starts to seem smug or dour or stick-up-the-butt-y. It feels like we're losing the forest for the trees. Where's the love, people?

When I first started practicing in my lineage, I had come from general American mindfulness, and I was baffled, and a bit put off, by the constant offerings to teachers and Buddhas—endless preparations of shrines, water bowls, fruits, flowers and, most confusing to me, all of the prostrating. It all felt inefficient and subservient to a mind well steeped in productivity and independence. It also felt beyond the call of duty. I paid my retreat fee—can't I just go to the sessions, get the goods and get on with it?

With some hesitation, I took part in not only the practices but also the offerings around them. Over time, I have found that the quiet practice of offering has perhaps shifted my mind and heart more than the obvious practices of meditation and the such. Working with offering has moved me from transactional mind to devotional mind and, wow, does that feel sublime.

Offering mind disrupts the self by focusing us fully on giving instead of taking. In fact, with its absence of attachment, offering goes beyond giving in the usual way we give. Most of our giving is transactional, controlling, codependent, martyrish—we expect something, even just gratitude or attention, in return for our so-called generosity. As we'll see, offering is an expression of delight in being here. It is the heart's celebration of interdependence. We are showing reverence for the whole miraculous situation. We are life giving to life. We are uncovering instantaneous meaning and use for our lives even in seemingly mundane moments.

Of course, this requires cultivation. The beauty of offering is that we can fake it until we make it. We've been trimming and uprooting the weeds of our self-centered, ignorant impulse to take by following the ethical precept of not taking what is not given and also contemplating interdependence. Now, we water our inherent seeds of wisdom, compassion and, most of all, joy through offerings of all kinds. Even if it feels a little forced at first, offering rains nourishment on our potential to delight in being alive—right here, right now, no matter what.

Before we talk about what we can offer, let's consider to what we are making our offerings. Because I practice Tantric Buddhism, I'm karmically dialed into feeling devotion and thus making offerings to teachers and Buddhas. That is not as creepy as it initially sounds to the less deferential Western mind. This path is nontheistic and nondual—so external teachers and Buddhas are also the teacher within and the Buddha you already are. Ironically, all of this external devotion and offering cultivates a healthy respect for one's own potential as a human being as well as the potential of all beings and our world. So we can offer to anything that represents the big picture potential of life—God, Gaia, the Universe, spaceship Earth, all our relations, future generations, all beings. To life, to life, l'chaim!

We have endless ways to offer throughout the day. For starters, we can offer our spiritual practice to be of benefit to our world. All too often, we approach spiritual practice—from meditation and prayer to ecstatic dance and shamanic healing—with a what's-in-it-for-me mentality. This makes sense because we are in pain and looking for a way out. However, unless our practice uproots what's-in-it-for-me, we'll always be in pain. Freedom lies in jettisoning the me-first mental state of taking, attaching, consuming, fixing, getting and changing. When we offer up our spiritual practice, we are feeding our generosity, openness, gratitude, contentment and joy, and this is what actually helps us feel better. We stop looking to use practice to boost our career or patch up our love life or get a bunch of money. We orient toward making use of our lives in whatever form suits the moment. My teachers always say that the best thing we can offer is diligent practice on behalf of others. Actually, making our practice an offering makes it easier to do our spiritual practice—we all know it's often easier to do things for others instead of ourselves. We can capitalize on this instinct to be of benefit by setting up our practice as an offering for others at the start and dedicating it as an offering for others at the end. Bookend practice as an offering—boom!

We can also have formal physical offerings, spiritual or not. I have a shrine with seven small water bowls, which I fill each morning as an offering to the Buddhas. Are the Buddhas thirsty? No. But my habitual mind is thirsty with thoughts of I, me, mine—ready to start the day in self-absorbed anxiety. So, instead, I open each morning with prostrations and filling the water bowls. These acts water seeds of appreciation for being alive yet another morning and reorient my mind and day toward being of service. We need not even own our offerings, so to speak. Throughout the day, as I pass by smiling flowers or a singing bird or the sounds of laughter or a pile of dog doo providing food for flies, I offer up those things too. Eventually, our background track of thoughts turns from harping on self-absorbed anxiety to noticing things to offer. We shift from fearing life to honoring life.

We can offer our work. Before we write emails or documents, before we start a meeting or teach a class, before we take a phone call, before we serve a customer, before we pick up our tools, before we care for our or others' children, we can make an offering of our actions. As mentioned in the previous chapter, I teach meditation at a living facility for individuals transitioning into stable housing. Many of them are working for the city on landscaping crews. This past week they were washing tulip bulbs all day. We talked about the brilliance of offering each tulip bulb, how we couldn't think of a more glorious offering, all of that splendor preparing to spring forth from the bulb. So, as we step into whatever our work may be, we make an offering that this writing or meeting or conversation or action or tulip bulb be of benefit to all beings, may it make the world a better place for my grandchildren, may it be a celebration of life. Suddenly, work of all kinds takes on a transcendent tone, and we consider anew how our work does affect our grandchildren and all beings.

We can offer things that we covet. Whenever I pass by desirable homes or clothes or bikes or things that I want, want, want, I offer them up. May that gorgeous home overlooking the mountains be of benefit to all who live there and all the rest of us. For whatever reason, I then feel joy over that home's existence instead of sadness that I don't live in it. Recently, I've even done this with a person. There's a new man in my life who is a person of interest, as they say. We don't live in the same place and we're battle-worn forty-somethings, so it's not clear what to do with this sweet affection and sexy attraction. The other day he called me from his family's home in a tropical locale. I heard birdsong in the background, and he explained that he was sunbathing naked in the garden— the man is a fan of vitamin D and apparently "it's good to get sun on the boys." My first and immediately expressed thought was, "What a delightful experience. I'm offering it to the Buddhas!" Later, I realized that offering mind left me relaxed and open in our conversation. An earlier iteration of me would have been all, "Why is he calling me naked, what's going on here," and become all obsessive, yearning and freaked out. None of that self-centered drama happened. I was simply pleased that he was enjoying himself—that's it. Offering reorients us from coveting to celebrating the loveliness in the world.

On a related note, we can offer relationships of all kinds. Beyond the garden moment, I offer our friendship all the time—may our connection help each of us be more wise, compassionate, joyful and useful to this world. Bingo—I'm at peace. With the why of our connection offered up, the details of what, where, when and how will sort themselves out. We can offer up conversations and entire relationships of the romantic, friend, family, neighbor, work variety. We then see the potential for co-creating something wonderful for our world in how we speak and behave with one another all the time.

We can offer perfect moments that are tinged with the sadness of impermanence. Even when everything is how we'd like it, there is always the reality that it is not going to last. So, there in the moment of awesome, we feel a bit of grasping and suffering. I notice this all the time when I'm hiking. I reach a spectacular summit, rest there in communion with this world that I am and that I love...and lingering in the back of my mind is melancholy that this moment will end. So I offer the vista, butterflies, happiness and moment to the Buddhas and all beings. Then, there is a sense that the moment is beyond me and my grasping. Our pleasure amplifies and extends out somehow, and we feel released from the pain of attachment.

We can offer difficult moments. Offering bestows purpose upon the inevitable occasions of pain and frustration in our lives. We simply offer that this time somehow be of benefit to ourselves and others. In some way, whether through lessons learned or karma cleared or however it happens, may our pain result in peace for self and other. Like so many of us, my mind tends to worry about money. Whenever I am in the thick of it, I say, "Okay, on behalf of all of us, I am going to be the one who worries about money for the next fifteen minutes. Everyone else take a break from it. I offer up my money worries to be of benefit to the whole team." Suddenly, the worry about money releases—because I've remembered that everyone out there is struggling with this worry and much more. My mind blooms with compassion for all of us because being human is hard. It's the isolation of anxiety that really hurts; offering brings us back into teamwork with humanity. It's not a wish to martyr oneself and bring on the pain for glory and attention. Rather, in our lowest moments, it's a quiet act of transmutation from loneliness and self-pity to connection and meaning.

We can offer our food, homes and clothes—the basics of life. However much or little we have, we can make these things nourishing and nurturing and give them as a gift to ourselves and the world. When the focus is being of benefit, as opposed to getting attention, inciting jealousy or capturing craving, there is freedom to discover what feels naturally elegant, as I have found with the offering of my appearance at retreat ceremonies. We humbly show respect for ourselves and others with how we engage on a physical level with the world. During a chapter of starving myself back in NYC, I looked scary. My face and body were sunken, tight, suffering. One day, I walked past a woman who winced upon seeing me. I had a flash of insight—I don't want my appearance to bring pain to others. Despite the obvious pain I was causing my family and friends, it was the look on that stranger's face that jolted my self-centered thoughts just enough to let in a little light. In making an offering of how we care for ourselves, we honor our current physical form and our world in ways that feel peaceful and true for us.

We can offer our workouts. This feels worth mentioning in our culture. One of my teachers once joked that if Americans spent half as much time on spiritual practice as we did on perfecting our bodies, we'd all be enlightened by now. Guilty as charged and then some. As someone who spent freshman year of college majoring in compulsive exercise, let me say that we can offer up our physical endeavors to be of benefit to all beings. This helps us consider why we are doing what we are doing, how it contributes to the world and how it might not. It also gives us a quick shot of thinking about others, which could mitigate a workout replete with self-absorption that painfully echoes into other parts of our lives.

We can offer moments of cool boredom. All of those everyday activities in life can become a gift. When we wash the dishes, walk to the store, call customer service, we can offer the experience to the highest potential of all parties involved, to the future of our children and the planet. This aspiration lends grace, dignity, even wonder to these seemingly small actions. We carry ourselves with greater purpose in all that we do. We appreciate that no act is too small to be of significance to our lives and the lives of others. We foster connection to others and our world constantly as we move through our seemingly mundane days.

Offering mind acknowledges that intention is everything. When we reorient the mind from what can I get to what can I give, the whole situation changes. Offering brings us into awareness of our surroundings, mental states and behavior with an eye seeking interdependence, beauty, resilience and hope. We don't need a perfect offering. We simply offer what is true for us right here and right now—it's all a rich display worthy of sharing.

Cultivating joy and gratitude through offering is a wildly rebellious act in a competitive, capitalist culture that trains us into thinking that nothing is ever enough, not me or you or anything about our situation. Through offering, our sense of self grows beyond a limited, defensive, shutdown posture to being open, available, generous and alive. We are life thoroughly in love with life. It's all so awesome, even the dog doo, I have to offer it up! Such joy is available to us all the time. It doesn't come from magic but from practice.

Experiment

- Choose a focus for offering—teachers, Buddhas, God, Gaia, the Universe, spaceship Earth, all our relations, future generations, all beings, life.
- Choose an area of life—spiritual practice, nature, work, things you covet, relationships and conversations, beauty, pain, food/homes/clothes, workouts, errands, cool boredom moments.
- For one day, commit to making offerings in this area of life. When you forget, no big deal. When you remember, start again.
- Notice changes in behaviors, thoughts, emotional and mental states.
- Try it for another day. And another.
- Try it with another area of life. And another.

Hope in Humanity

After my flight back from my Stanford MBA reunion, I was immersed in graduation events and grading papers for Naropa University where I received my MDiv and where I'd spent the semester teaching courses on Life, Work and Authenticity as well as Social Innovation and Entrepreneurship. While I was treated to extraordinary educations and soulful communities at both schools, I often reflect on the slight difference in their mottos and thus intentions. Stanford's Graduate School of Business tells us to "Change lives. Change organizations. Change the world." Thanks to Naropa's Buddhist origins, it tells us to "Transform Yourself. Transform the World." It's a call to personal responsibility. It asks us to examine and transform the mind and thus self before we jump into changing this or that—otherwise all of that supposed change is really more of the same because it is simply a new expression of habitual patterns.

We often talk about how technology, money and such

tools are neutral. We can use them to lift us up or drag us down. We like this argument because then we can keep using social media or capitalism or whatever and tell ourselves that we're using it consciously and for good. Sometimes that seems on point. Other times, we look at our phones and know that for any good they might do they were still created by and for a mind that is terrified to be with itself; we look at so-called conscious capitalism and see a mind still habitually driven toward more, more, more. We start to see that there's a certain mind behind most of our tools and even our supposed innovations—and it is often a mind geared toward taking instead of giving. If we want to truly innovate as a culture and world, we need to transform the mind behind our creations.

So we take stock of our minds and use mental tools that have been proven to wake people up—tools of ethics, contemplation and offering that help us leave the prison of me-first consumption and move into a web of reciprocity. We look at our long-standing, claustrophobic, competitive survival mind—and we use the ethic of not taking what is not given to trim those weeds. Culturally, we own up to collectively training in ignorant individualism—and we contemplate and act from interdependence to rip those weeds out at the root. Together, we admit that we want more connection and care from and for ourselves, each other and this world—and we cultivate offering mind to grow our inherent seeds of wisdom, compassion and especially joy. If we commit to this kind of practice, what kind of world might we grow?

Sitting on that airplane, it felt like we were losing our potential as humans. It wasn't only the masturbating over FaceTime—on some level I get it, girl; my person of interest is at a distance too. It was that the entire plane felt like it was masturbating, the way it feels these days like we're all masturbating all the time—often buried in screens, always lost in daydreams, thinking about a future when we finally get what we want, still never being satisfied even if we get it. Then we wonder why we feel isolated and sad. Not to knock masturbation, but it doesn't really satisfy. As humans, we want intercourse—we seek union with each other and our world. We don't just want to take; we also want to give. We want a sensual, passionate, intimate connection with each other and life itself. We want to be hands-in-hair, legs-intertwined, caught-up-in-the-moment ALIVE. We want to be in love with life.

If we want to get love, we need to give love. What is a greater expression of love for self, other and the world than reorienting from what can I get to what can I give? When we drop consumption mind and step into offering mind, we express a fearless love of life. We turn back toward each other and see that it is only through relationship that we release painful selfishness. We leave behind our culture's entitlement—no longer thinking that life owes us something and instead wondering what we might offer life. We acknowledge the reality of our interdependence and take responsibility for creating our future in the present. The center of innovation is the mind. What might we create when we stop seeing ourselves as consumers and remember that we are humans? We have tremendous potential to birth communion and joy among ourselves. Nothing external required. What we are seeking is already within us and between us. We need only extend our humanity.

Winning is a State of Mind
Not Harming Living Beings

America. Another day, another divisive political drama. This latest one was a big one—the intersection of the #MeToo movement with the Supreme Court hearings when a woman accused the male nominee of sexually assaulting her when they were in high school. After the votes were tallied, a reporter asked the president about the wake of division this episode had left behind and he replied, "It doesn't matter. We won." And I thought, "Who's we? Who's they? And what's winning?"

Here's a hint at what's not winning—hunkering down into categories of we, they and winning. Like the president and many of us, I was experiencing a massive hit of that afflictive, alienating mental state. In the spirit of sticking to a healthy mental diet, I keep strong boundaries around media and social media. Get in and get out. Stay informed but don't wallow. Until these Supreme Court hearings, when I chugged the news cycle and chased it with Facebook. Immediately and increasingly, my mind became tight, repetitive, claustrophobic—stuck on poor me and eff you. Like so many people on the planet—dare I say all women—I've had my share of unwanted sexual experiences and harassment ranging from annoying to terrifying. And it all rose to the surface. And I wasn't alone in that. As has often been the case the past few years, it was hellish but perhaps helpful to see our stuff bubble up in a trigger fest of division and anger. It felt like no matter where we stood on the hearings, we were fracturing into we and they and who's winning.

In my pain, my mind made all men THEY and I was done with them. And, logically, I knew that not all men perpetuate such pain. But, emotionally, I was stuck in poor me and eff them. I could barely look at men. I didn't even want to hear male voices. I shut out my person of interest. I avoided male friends. I hoped my mom would answer instead of my dad. On a trail one afternoon, I passed some dude as he delivered a monologue to his date, and the entire mountain, about the hearings, and he scoffed that "she wasn't even raped." Possessed by anger, I fantasized about becoming ginormous, attacking him as if to anally rape him and then seeing how he felt about *not even* being raped...or pulling out my bloody menstrual pad and sticking it on his chest with creepy eye contact...or suddenly flying and raining menstrual blood upon him and all the land, bwahaha. And that swarm of thoughts left me tired and more upset. A few minutes later, I was walking behind two men, one of whom was wearing a t-shirt with a joke about blondes on it. For five steps or so, I gave them the middle finger mudra behind their backs, feeling stupid and not any better for it.

After the hike, I was headed into Natural Grocers and sensed that the hipster in hemp pants by the bike rack was going to say something to me. Feeling zero tolerance, I inhabited all of my being to breeze by him. Still, he moved into my sight line, smirked and said, "You'll feel a lot better if you smile." In response to my silence and stride, he trailed after me with a taunting, "Really, try smiling sometime." I'll admit that I called on every bit of my vows and practice not to unleash the beast all over that guy. Even still, there was an undercurrent of violence between us. Here we were—a meditation teacher in barefoot shoes and a bike commuter in breathable fabrics, respectively pre and post quinoa purchase in the sunniest city in the land, sporting shared white privilege and enough coin to buy organic and probably a common voting record—and it felt like imminent fisticuffs. Over what? His catcall laced with love and light shaming? My aura of anger? At that point, I thought, "This is not winning, woman."

I recognized that, while trapped in the pain of poor me,

I was causing a bit of harm toward others but mostly myself. The harm was seemingly minor in its outward expression, but I was watering seeds for worse, doing nothing to dismantle the patriarchy and feeling physically and mentally miserable. I was indulging in anger, which I do a lot. I mean, you don't get into the meditation business because everything's going great with the whole thinking thing. And, all too often, it's not going great for any of us. Despite our specific personal and social circumstances, we are all like-minded in that the human mind is a habitual minefield often leaving us feeling alone, angry and all too ready to cause harm.

It gets confusing though, doesn't it, around issues of injustice. Because the harm we experience and inflict on the basis of sex, gender, sexuality, race, ethnicity, age, ability, beliefs, differences of all kinds is worthy of inspiring anger. In fact, a flash of anger can be clarifying—a gut signal on boundaries, letting us know that this is not how we or others should be treated. Yet, trained in self-interest, we take that signal and reduce it to the personal. "That shouldn't happen" turns into "that shouldn't happen *to me*"—as if we are the only ones in pain. Our insights get sucked down the drain of self-pity, and we lose perspective on how our mutual pain is actually a point of human connection that we can leverage for healing. The great teachers of nonviolent resistance always speak to the interdependence of injustice—how oppressor and oppressed are only freed together. Okay in theory, but how do we live in that space of union? How do we train our minds so that we act from the space of knowing we are only free if we are all free? How do we drop our habitual distraction of seeking division that perpetuates a harm-filled cycle of hate and violence where nobody wins?

In the spirit of freedom, in this chapter, we'll reveal and release our mental tendency to divide, which is what creates personal suffering and social injustice. To do so, we'll look at the ethic of not harming living beings in three ways. First, we'll use the ethic as a path to notice and stop at least some of the ways we harm living beings. This is like trimming the weeds. Next, we'll explore the ethic as a contemplation on selflessness, which is not a negation of our existence but an awareness of our existence as being bigger than our stories of self and identity, stories that perpetuate pain, division and harm. This is like pulling the weeds out at the root. Finally, we'll expand on the ethic to experiment with the energetic experience of selflessness or transcendent moments of nondualism. This is like giving water and sunshine to our inherent seeds of wisdom, compassion and joy.

To briefly geek out in Buddhist terms, we will aspire to grow our wisdom from the relative to the absolute, building on our exploration of interdependence in the last chapter with an exploration of selflessness in this chapter. This insight of wisdom—into interdependence and then selflessness—is referred to as the feminine principle in Buddhism because it births our compassionate action, which is the masculine principle. These principles inherently and energetically exist within us, having nothing to do with sex or gender. We are each so much larger than self-identity, and we can grow beyond it to free us all.

Not Harming Living Beings— Try on the Mind of Loving Them

After years of wanting to take refuge vows—a ceremony that marks turning to Buddhist teachings and practices for life's answers and adopting the ethical precepts—I finally did so in a Tantric Buddhist lineage that felt more Tibetan, traditional and formal than I'd anticipated for myself. How I ended up there is a whole other story involving prophecy, obstacles and miracles. As we know, the greatest offerings we give and receive often come with obstacles and miracles and perhaps a dash of prophecy. Entering this path within this lineage meant taking on the aforementioned, massive set of preliminary practices called ngöndro, which begins with 100,000 prostrations. I had a thick skeptic story around prostrations that included I don't bow down to anything thank you very much. Yet, it felt choiceless. So I began.

To start, I went to retreat with my lineage for the first time where I recognized the teacher of prior prophecy. There, in this traditional setting singing prayers and practices in transliterated Tibetan, I was of two minds—this is too foreign, complicated, ceremonial, patriarchal for me…and I have been reunited with all of my favorite songs may I please never stop singing them. Shortly before taking refuge, I had a meeting with my teacher. There was a lot of formality and protocol that was intimidating and irritating to my perfectionist and entitled mind. As instructed, I prepared my one question on a piece of paper, walked down a dirt road to the teacher's house, waited in line and was ushered in to sit before him with another teacher to serve as a translator. The experience of meeting him was ineffable, and we'll get there in the third part of this chapter. His response to my prepared question was humbling, and we'll get there in the second part of this chapter. The curveball came after he'd answered my carefully prepared question and the translating teacher told me I had time for another. It was a reverse pop quiz and what popped out of my mouth was, "Why do prostrations make me so angry?" The translator laughed. He translated the question and my teacher laughed. Later, I told an older retreat friend about this and he also laughed. I asked him why everyone was laughing and he said, "You don't look like an angry person." Oh, but aren't we all?

After his sweet laugh, my teacher said that human beings have a lot of pride, the false pride of ego. Prostrations—to one's inherent wisdom—are an antidote to pride and cutting through that stirs up our anger. It's like ego withdrawal syndrome. The conscious commitment to not harm living beings also cuts through egoic pride, sans prostrations. Pride is self-centered.

When life inevitably doesn't go as planned, we get offended and want to harm what we perceive to be in our way. We get angry with people but also with flies or inanimate objects. Working with the ethic of not harming living beings cuts egoic pride and anger because we reroute the mind to look at life from another being's perspective. Not harming living beings is absolutely about respecting other beings, but it is also training the mind to release the grip of pride and anger.

Most of us have been attempting to not harm human beings our entire lives, and, of course, we will discuss humans in a moment. However, this ethic is about not harming all living beings, so it widens our circle of consideration. When actively employing this ethic, an obvious and visceral way to stop harming living beings is to stop killing bugs. Many who take these vows take this step, as did I—a lifelong bug killer who was especially scared of spiders, all those legs, please be gone. Boulder's not the buggiest place, but my vows coincided with moving into a 100-year-old house that was not so tightly sealed. And, oh, the spiders. Spiders as big as your fist. Spiders that, when you lie down, make a quick trip across your neck, breast, belly, inner thigh. Spider babies rappelling from the ceiling like the final scene of *Charlotte's Web*. Right away, I saw how making an actual vow to not harm living beings makes a difference in one's mind because I woman'ed up and became an expert in catch and release. To alleviate my fear, I tried fake it till you make it friendliness—"Hello, friend, you are too big to live inside...I don't want to harm you...help me help you."

Then, one day, we find that there's no need to fake it. When we stop harming these little beings, we become more relaxed about them. Instead of being upset that a bug has spoiled our plans to not see a bug, we see that bugs are simply trying to live and not suffer. Bugs—they're just like us! So we live and let live with the spider in the corner. We even develop curious appreciation through catch and release as we learn how moths, millipedes, mosquitoes all move and live differently. We might even discover warmth and affection for bugs, which always feels better than fright and aversion. Silly as it sounds, our world gets less lonely. Recently, I had a difficult-to-catch fly live with me for a day in my no-pets apartment. I named him Bob and sang mantras to him, eventually ushering him out so he could fulfill his fly destiny. There are so many bug friends to appreciate when we are walking or waiting at the corner. Each time we pay loving attention to them, we reroute the mind off of pride's mantra of *what about me*.

Actually, from a Buddhist point of view, that bug and I have the same potential for enlightenment—contemplating our basic equality with ants can also help erode egoic pride. Even if we don't want to go there, we still get mental benefits when we stop harming even some bugs. Again, I'm in the high desert and fairly bug free. My parents live in the coastal Southeast, and none of us want what are euphemistically named palmetto bugs—giant roaches—in our food or hair or anywhere. So there's a balance to find with insects that involves safety and hygiene. Even if we commit to not harming some bugs, we'll notice that we become less reactive and violent in general. These most dissimilar beings offer an opportunity to develop the mind's ability to shift from irritation and fear to ease and friendliness in the face of difference.

This method continues with not harming animals, and this arena holds serious potential for training our minds in love. Many of us have had a beloved pet in our day, and our love for that animal is pure. Our pet's vulnerability and innocence are heartbreaking; their signals of gratitude and companionship are humbling. As if caring for an infant or child, we do our best not to harm that animal, and we reap rewards from that. It feels wonderful to love something that simply. The thing is, there are a lot of animals around us, not just the ones we actively care for. They are also vulnerable, innocent, relatable beings and available for love.

There are many ways in which we harm animals through our consumption of the planet. The most immediate and personal ways we harm animals are eating them and wearing them. Everyone has their own choices to make around eating animals—people's bodies have different needs, and cultures have different customs. Similarly, everyone has their own choices to make around wearing animals. We also have choices to make around protecting ourselves from animals; that safety and hygiene issue arises again. But, I will share this nugget of personal experience. There have been a lot of reasons for my not eating animals over the years such as health, vanity and the environment. Yet, when the primary reason became non-harming, a few noteworthy things happened. First, it was much easier to not eat animals or animal products, so I saw the mind's preference for doing things on behalf of others. I also had some sobering ego contemplation on whether my fleeting sensory pleasure of taste or even my supposed optimal health/attractiveness was more important than another being's life or well-being. Further, there was a love explosion. I had not realized my cognitive dissonance around loving animals while arbitrarily eating some of them. With that out of the way, my mind and heart were free to love them all, even the ones that scare me sometimes, and by that I mean mice more than mountain lions. We feel better when we have something to love, especially in an uncomplicated way; we know this from studies on the benefits of pets. As with bugs, there are countless animals around us every day. This means countless opportunities for the mind to travel down a path of love as opposed to ruminating on pride's mantra of *what about me*. When we stare out the window, instead of thinking about ourselves, we can love up the squirrel who loves to feel the warmth of the sun just like us.

Interestingly, training within the less familiar, through bugs and animals, may help us recognize our impetus to harm human beings. Simply put, we notice our instinct to prioritize self over other. With bugs and animals, we see how such egoic pride leads to harming beings through stark actions of killing or eating them—and the love that flows from releasing this cycle. Within our more complicated relationships of the human family, our egoic pride takes on subtler and more complex tricks of prioritizing self over other. Yet, just like us, our human siblings are also trying to live and not suffer despite our varied, confused, even destructive strategies around this. Rather than getting angry about or even fearing such differences between us, our minds can develop a genuine gentleness such that it feels not only inhumane but also inhuman to harm anyone in any form.

However, we have to truly reckon with this because we habitually harm each other almost constantly. It is easy to think that we're not harming humans if we aren't physically hurting people. And, of course, not physically hurting people is included in this ethic. But there's more to it than that. We can notice and release angry, harmful thoughts we think about others, be it people we know, strangers we pass, those in the media or on social media—seeing how such thoughts pollute our minds and environment. There is also cleaning up the way we talk to and about people—there's a reason cursing is called cursing—and the next chapter is entirely devoted to speech because it's a major way we interact with and harm each other. Further, we can contemplate harming others just as we considered stealing from others; meaning we allow ourselves to see immediate and far-reaching effects of our varying aspects of privilege.

When I walk my beloved Boulder mountains and expand my sense of self to include this place, my hikes have origins in the stolen land and forced, violent removal of the Arapaho people. My non-animal, plant-based meals contain the results of harming many people, often disproportionately people of color, who are toiling for a non-living wage in various parts of the supply chain. My taking career risks as a white person with faith that I can land on my feet has roots in our country's wealth and education gap, which is built on the slave labor, torture and discriminatory abuse of Black people, even children, throughout time. My many freedoms as an American, including practicing this spiritual practice, come at the cost of countless human lives damaged by and lost to war. So, I must consider, what are ways through my relationship with this place and land, through my purchasing choices, through the fruits of my opportunities, through my spiritual practice that I can contribute to the cessation of harming all of these beautiful human beings. Do not be fooled by my praying with flies and eye gazing with squirrels; I have a tremendous amount of work to do with this ethic of non-harming. Honestly, it feels impossible to live a human life without generating or benefiting from harm of other human beings, especially as an American and a white person and someone with several additional categories of privilege such as having higher education and being straight and cisgender. My simply taking up space in spaces can be harmful to others.

Though the seeming impossibility of not harming human beings is never a reason not to try. With our growing understanding of interdependence, we see that there are countless verbal, emotional, physical, political and economic choices that could honor rather than harm our human siblings. Imagine the release of cognitive dissonance if we acted in ways that acknowledged all humans are available for love; imagine how much less lonely we would feel and how much we would learn. We can start again and again by looking at life as an opportunity to not harm other humans but instead fearlessly love them, all of them, no matter how hard that seems—which eradicates pride's mantra of *what about me* to reveal empathy and expressions thereof.

Of course, love and empathy often require a fierce energy. In a world where we habitually act out our pain on each other, not harming beings, including not turning our back on the harming of beings, requires saying big NO's internally, interpersonally and systemically. We need to set personal and political boundaries on behalf of self and/or other. Our awareness of the need to set a boundary usually begins with a flash of anger, our intuitive signal of violation. However, skillfully maintaining healing boundaries requires fierceness or wrath, as it is sometimes named in the Buddhist tradition. Using this verbiage, the difference between wrath and anger is that wrath is inspired by love and a desire to cease the cycle of harm, while anger gets gummed up by egoic pride and leaves us in further pain and division.

Many moons before #MeToo, I got to know anger and wrath well when I reported sexual harassment within a cherished community. Though my claim prevailed, the experience included a confusing investigation process and insidious retaliation, all of which felt violating as well. Throughout, I watched my mind oscillate between anger and wrath, and I learned that wrath is a cleaner-burning fuel.

Anger feels small, tight, panicked, fearful and all too ready to fight because it is characterized by egoic pride and taking the situation personally, which I tend to do with gender issues. Most of us tend to take harm personally and why wouldn't we? Harm hurts mentally, emotionally and physically, even more so when we have endured a lifetime of personal harm founded upon collective historical harm. My initial anger around the harm was a healthy alarm system; the trouble was when it stuck around. I went from being victimized to identifying as a victim, and we know how different those states are. The latter is fueled by egoic pride because the situation becomes all about *what about me*.

With time, perspective and practice, I felt my mind gravitate toward wrath, which was clear, strong, quiet, connected and generative. The more I maintained boundaries—boundaries on behalf of my being as well as boundaries on self's egoic pride—the more space I had to consider the complexity of the interdependent situation. I saw the intersecting pain and confusion of all parties involved, extending beyond the main actors to the larger community. Accordingly, I saw the comprehensiveness of compassion. First, I understood what all parents know—compassion includes accountability. It's how we learn and move forward. Of course, this may include our own accountability, even when we are victimized and harmed. Part of not harming beings could be recognizing ways we harm ourselves and others by giving up our intrinsic human power, which remains untainted and personally available despite structural disempowerment. For me, in this instance, dropping my pride and anger and shifting into wrath included stepping out of that victim position, only to discover opportunities to reclaim my strength and sanity in this situation and moving forward. Moreover, I appreciated the multitude of compassionate actions one could take to decrease harm, depending on safety, power and privilege—such as boldly speaking truth to power, supporting the physical and emotional resilience of the victimized and marginalized, promoting awareness and education around instances of harm, encouraging rest and rejuvenation to deescalate stress and conflict. I saw there were many ways to wisely untie knots of habitually and historically compounded confusion in order to make the community safer for everyone, and in no way was this all about me—which meant that thankfully I wasn't alone in any of it.

Not harming living beings, especially human beings, is a significant ethical endeavor. Again, hurt people hurt people, and we are all hurt people. Breaking our habitual patterns of harming each other cuts to the core of our anger and egoic pride around human pain and self-pity. Working with this ethic, we can see that, even in our stickiest places of pain, when we think and act on behalf of all parties and humanity overall, we feel release and potential.

After my day of mountain madness, I appreciated that post-vows it felt strange to be besieged by the small scope of egoic pride. And it was interesting that such anger was now less familiar to me, especially around gender. Because gender is the area where I have experienced the most harm in my life, that issue fires up an angry egoic pride that wants to harm others, if only with angry thoughts. That is the self-pity that can lead us into harmful speech and action, and I know it well. Yet, it seems I know that state less well these days after exploring this ethic without even setting the intention of undoing that particular pattern.

Because the truth is, I don't want to cancel men any more than I want to cancel spiders. Sure, there are differences in how we move and live. And, I don't want some of them in my space—again, safety and hygiene. But, by and large, men are not causing me harm. Indeed, men have been a great comfort and support to me as brothers, friends and lovers. Men, spiders and I all have our role in the ecosystem. Granted that ecosystem includes patriarchy, a system that is extremely harmful for all sexes and genders alike. However, I'm not going to solve that problem by being angry with every guy momentarily displaying ignorance rooted in patriarchal socialization.

In fact, it is only through compassionate and curious connections, including boundaries, that we cease harming each other, practice loving each other and create lasting change. Besides, if men no longer existed, women would simply find ways to divide and harm each other—oh, wait, we do that all the time already. So it's not hard to see that the real enemy is the mind that creates division, which fuels egoic pride, anger and harm. And the mind is where we're headed next. But, by starting with the basic discipline to not harm living beings, we once again do an about-face on self-interest—when we expand our focus beyond ourselves, we actually feel much better.

Experiment

- With the next bug you spot in your space, try leaving it alone or catching and releasing it. You can use a glass to trap it, slide a piece of paper underneath and then release it outside with, "Be free!" Try it for a whole week.

- When you are outside, look down to see if there are any bug friends. Say hello, watch how they move, consider their day.

- Speak to your pet in an even softer, kinder voice. Hang out in silence and speak mind to mind. Consider what they want most from the day—warmth, food, love—and how special it is to give that to them.

- Smile at animals outside as if they were beloved pets. Watch how they move and live. Consider what they want most from the day—warmth, food, love—and make a wish that they have that.

- Experiment with eating/using fewer animals and animal products. Each time you do eat/use animals, think about the lives involved and say a prayer of thank you.

- Notice the subtle or not so subtle thoughts about harming other humans. Each time they occur, simply take a breath and recognize that they are impermanent thoughts that will move on. Let them go over and over again.

- Notice what happens if you refrain from harsh or harmful language—internally and externally—especially when it comes to people with whom you disagree.

- Consider the ways in which certain actions, purchases, behaviors, votes may have ripple effects that harm others. Set an intention to cease that harm and see what other options arise.

- Through education, explore ripple effects of various aspects of privilege—there are countless resources online, in books and in our communities about the experiences of marginalized individuals and groups. Whether we have privilege in some forms or are marginalized in some forms, there are a lifetime's worth of opportunities to listen and thus learn about the potentially harmful effects of our thoughts, speech and actions on others. And thus there are a lifetime's worth of opportunities to make changes that cultivate love instead.
- Get real about whether you are physically harming other humans directly and set an intention to stop. Get help if needed. Notice the effect on the mind from ceasing the pattern of physical harm.
- Recognize places where you allow the harm of others and make an intention to set personal and/or political boundaries. See what ideas arise when supporting a cycle of help rather than harm.
- Recognize ways in which you contribute to harming yourself, either through not caring for yourself properly or tolerating situations where you are harmed. Set an intention to shift that pattern, explore resources to help you and notice if strength emerges to help you free all parties involved in the cycle.

Not Harming Living Beings—
Piercing the Project of Me

The connection to one's primary teacher is vital to Tantric Buddhism because it is a path of devotion. As I walked down the dirt road to my teacher's house, I wondered how strong a connection I could make with someone who didn't really know me. At the time, my mind thought someone knowing me meant they knew my story, particulars about my life, my accomplishments and experiences. How could this teacher be my guide to freedom if he didn't know anything about me or even my name? Though this path felt choiceless, I felt doubt. So I asked him, in my carefully prepared question, how to work with such doubt in a process and path that felt so unfamiliar. He opened his response by saying that right now my mind was small. I felt an instinctive flash of offense—um, I went to Harvard—and immediately recognized my small mind right there. Thus began a process of seeing how much we limit ourselves with our concepts of our selves. The long list of things we think about ourselves is actually a prison of sorts—the prison of the project-of-me. Even worse, this project-of-me creates divisions between us, on small and large scales, which lead to personal unrest and social injustice. That said, because of the direct link between personal pain and collective pain, as we free ourselves we also free each other.

Where we're heading may initially feel harsh. People are generally fine with the feminine principle's insight into interdependence; it's common sense really. However, when she starts messing with our selves—especially in our culture of individualism—well, shut the front door. Fortunately, the feminine principle is unfazed by our fear; she is only interested in our freedom. She's often depicted as wild and naked, dancing on top of a corpse—a visual of fiercely and fearlessly trampling egoic pride. She's a master of wrath rooted in love, and she's not afraid of roughing up our selves to save our lives. And, remember, her insight is inherent to us all. Underneath our stories, our minds are pure wisdom.

Last chapter, we talked about interdependence—our indelible connection to the planet and each other, the endless links between all that is. Now, we consider what that means about each thing involved in this immense confluence of existence. For example, the table upon which my computer sits is made up of many components such as wood and metal. Those components are made up of elements like sun, water, soil, air. There are also contributing human hands and minds that gathered and coalesced the components and then designed, created, marketed, shipped and sold it all in table form. The original owners cared for it, then put it on the street where I found it, and my ex-boyfriend trimmed the legs so I could sit on the floor with it. All of those humans, from the loggers to my ex-boyfriend, existed and functioned thanks to food grown by others, people who cared for them and so on. And one day this table will break down and become another form, touching human, animal and plant life. This table as it exists right now is a momentary intersection of many causes and conditions. It is not a solid, separate or permanent entity. Nothing is. For the sake of convenience, we tag it with the label of table; but there's much more there. In Buddhism, this realization that everything is full of everything else is referred to as emptiness or selflessness. Things are empty of a separate self because they are full of countless causes and conditions coming together to create this momentary form. We can contemplate the selflessness of everything in the world, from houses to plants to animals to you and me.

The insight into the selflessness of oneself is essential to the absolute realization of the feminine principle's wisdom. To take steps there, we pay attention to our path. Practicing cool boredom invites awareness that our dramatic journey of life-death-space-life is just a free-flowing river of this leads to that. Contemplating interdependence invites awareness that myriad people, events and materials enable our being, growing, learning, living, dying. We see how we ourselves are an immense confluence of existence, created by countless cascades of causes and conditions coming together anew each moment. And so too is everything in the ever-changing ocean of all of life-death-space-life. We're fluid, dynamic and interconnected. It is only because of our emptiness of a solid, separate, permanent self that we even exist.

Still, like tagging the table with a label for the sake of convenience, we get a name as well. Are your parents going to call you the constantly changing confluence of the countless cascades of causes and conditions that enable you to be, grow, learn, live, die? It would be an awfully long Twitter handle. More than a name, we get a story. Or we create one. Being fluid, dynamic and interconnected is gorgeous but groundless, and we like to organize ourselves for participation in humanity. So we live our lives creating the project-of-me, a self, an identity, a story and the such. This meaning-making can help us process the human experience. However, the snafu is that we forget the reality of selflessness and instead become intoxicated with the project-of-me. It becomes habitual and entertaining, and we believe it to be the whole of us when it is simply a story that could be told a zillion different ways. Indeed, depending on our moods, we tell ourselves different versions of our stories of our selves all the time. The project-of-me is mercurial and not to be trusted as truth.

The habit of the project-of-me starts with our base impulse of "I want this but not that," which we dress up in ego's finery of "because I'm like this but not like that." It becomes instinctive albeit subtle to constantly cultivate a story of self and then campaign for ourselves and others to believe it. The dance between poor me and perfect me is part of it, but the project-of-me is much more than that. We habitually view everything in relation to our story of self and make our lives into performance pieces of "I'm like this but not like that." Actually, social media, as a concentrated example, helps us see the confusion in this project-of-me. We curate an online project-of-me knowing that it's limited and, furthermore, fake; but so too is our mental project-of-me that we're posting to all day. We are all different people throughout our lives, in different situations, with different interactions, day to day, moment by moment. We are verbs, not nouns. We are a selfless stream of experience. In our emptiness, we contain multitudes. Yet, thinking it will help us feel safe and happy in an uncertain and complex world, we habitually dumb ourselves down into this protective project-of-me.

Our tried-and-true tool in the project-of-me is the creation-of-you. The CliffsNotes version of me is "not you." You're like this, but I'm like that. Of course, more entertaining than difference is superiority and inferiority. You're like this, but I'm like *all* that. You're like this, but I'm like *only* that. With the project-of-me-creation-of-you, we reduce everyone else to our supporting cast of superior and inferior characters, and scorekeeping begins. Once we look for it, we see it. As a woman, I watch myself instinctively check out every woman who passes me for a quick superiority/inferiority check based on weight, attractiveness, clothes, age and apply it to the project-of-me. As a friend, I can listen to my friends talk about their lives while doing a running superiority/inferiority comparison on my life choices and apply it to the project-of-me. As a grocery shopper, I might notice the purchases of the folks around me and do a superiority/inferiority judgment on our eating and apply it to the project-of-me. It's a mental habit of dividing me from you in an attempt to get a handle on me.

Yet, the dualism of me-you is pretty lonely and still groundless with just me and all of these you's, so we take our favorite and/or most obvious me-you categories to build we-they. We're like this, but they're like that. Our family is like this, but that family is like that. Our school is like this, but that school is like that. Our city is like this, but that city is like that. Our football team is like this, but that football team is like that. Women are like this, but men are like that. Black people are like this, but white people are like that. Straight people are like this, but gay people are like that. Transgender people are like this, but cisgender people are like that. Urban people are like this, but rural people are like that. Republicans are like this, but Democrats are like that. Americans are like this, but Tibetans are like that. On and on. In this way, our stories of superiority and inferiority get bigger, become socialized and internalized, and take on serious significance as we use perceived difference to structure differences in economic, social and political power, not to mention basic human rights.

The project-of-me fails us on two levels: it's not real and it causes harm. My socialization as a white woman has meant the internalization of cultural stories of superiority based on race and inferiority based on gender. Yet, such stories are bogus. First, dualistic notions, such as me-you, we-they, superior-inferior, are but thoughts—subjective, fleeting, insubstantial mental activities appearing and disappearing in a conditioned chain reaction to each other—which have as much reality as a mirage. They are habits, not truths. Likewise, categories, such as white and woman, have no solid, separate, permanent existence. Case in point, humans have changed the definition of white people throughout history to keep economic and political power for some but not others. There are as many ways to be a woman as there are women. Still, the categories of white and woman have shaped my self, thanks to socially constructed opinions and opportunities and resultant internal beliefs. And this is only part of my ongoing, ignorant project-of-me, the likes of which intoxicates us all. Though we inherently know that this entire display of life is interdependent and each aspect of it is empty in its fullness of everything else, we keep building our selves, relationships and societies with imaginary thoughts. We are entranced by the mirage.

Moreover, this mirage creates great harm internally and externally. On the internal level, we think the project-of-me is going to ground us, but it ends up trapping us. The project-of-me feeds egoic pride. Whether me-you or we-they, we set up each scene with ourselves as the lead—yet that leaves us feeling discontent. We feel alone even threatened; we get defensive and hole up into our categories. We lose touch with our insight into and place within the web of life. The glorious complexity and connection of the human condition all too often collapses into poor me and eff you. Fueled by such painful thinking, on the external level, we then let fly words and actions that create the harm of personal unrest and social injustice. Throughout time, we cling to the ignorance of superior and inferior, oppressor and oppressed that robs us of our full humanity and potential as interconnected beings.

Because of the momentum and magnitude of these harmful personal and social patterns, it can all feel beyond our control. However, the roots of these weeds are within, and we can pull them out by working with our minds. With a bit of consistent effort, we can uproot the project-of-me. We do this humbly and honestly by being aware of our thoughts that divide us from others—the thoughts of comparison, criticism, judgment. Of course, we pay close attention to our fabricated, socialized stories around categories of societal division and discrimination—our superior/inferior stories about gender, sex, sexuality, race, ethnicity, education, ability, political party, religion, age, weight, occupation, income level and so on. But we also curb this destructive habit by flagging any more than/ less than comparison, criticism, judgment in the project-of-me-creation-of-you—like grocery purchases, exercise habits, home decor, fashion sense, relationship history, reading lists, musical preferences, moon signs, power animals, personality types, retirement plans, really anything. We notice how we create big and small stories of superiority and inferiority in order to grasp at an illusory ground of self and other in our groundless existence of interdependent selflessness—and we learn to let such stories be, thought by thought. All of this requires becoming familiar with the insubstantiality of thoughts. When we leave thoughts be, we see them arise and dissipate. We become less attached to their content, and we feel greater space in the whole situation of being human among humans.

To be clear, releasing the project-of-me-creation-of-you does not mean discounting the results of these thoughts and stories. That's the spiritual bypass move of misunderstanding emptiness as avoidance of interpersonal pain and social injustice with an irresponsible attitude of "hey, man, it's all good; we're all one." When we spiritually bypass and fail to address the pain and injustice of our divisions, we perpetuate the cycle of harm. So the contemplative work of releasing the project-of-me-creation-of-you is done in tandem with the active ethic of not harming living beings. We seek to prevent and redress interpersonal pain as well as social injustice while also growing wiser by seeing that the real enemy is the mind of division. As Buddhist teachers say, we keep our view as vast as the sky and our conduct as fine as barley flour.

As a woman, this has meant not simply replacing stories of discouragement with stories of empowerment but continually releasing the gender story generator entirely. It's like going beyond "go girl" to "let it go, girl." That way, while still actively protesting harmful gender socialization and discrimination, I also uncover more freedom of mind and thus openness to unlimited ways of being embodied—for self and all others. Additionally, digging deeper into the roots of stories helps clarify the compromised humanity on all sides of division. For example, we see how patriarchy gives men systemic power but cock-blocks them from inner powers of compassion, creativity, vulnerability, communication, tenderness, playfulness, connection, humility, not knowing, magic and on and on. We see how the regenerating horrors wrought by white supremacy have been perpetuated by white people's minds that are plagued by greed, violence, hate, fear, arrogance, pity, entitlement, condescension, confusion, ignorance, disregard and on and on. We feel all of our pain in the confused project-of-me-creation-of-you. Our hearts break open into compassion, which is the masculine principle in Buddhism. The feminine with her insight into the wisdom of selflessness births the masculine of compassion. So, rather than isolating in anger and causing further harm, we feel a fierce urgency to cease the project-of-me for us all.

However, as we release the project-of-me, there's a note of caution. As we've seen, the thinking mind latches onto binaries: poor me-perfect me, me-you, we-they. So, when dropping the project-of-me, it's easy for the mind to slip into the pit of nonexistence and meaninglessness. I know of what I speak. While there are many causes and conditions that have led to my self-annihilation tendencies, one of them is swinging from the project-of-me into the pit-of-nothing. Indeed, the first time the eating disorder reared its head was the first time I had some insights into the project-of-me. I'd arrived at Northwestern, and, like any of us when we leave home for the first time, I recognized the opportunity to reinvent oneself. People try on different personalities, styles of dress, interests, relationships in a search for that authentic self—the holy grail of individualist culture. Instead of feeling excited, I felt tired. It was too much effort to create Katie Malachuk all over again in any form. There was a flicker of insight that we are creating ourselves, this is an active pursuit, and there might be another way to experience life. However, I had not encountered teachings on interdependence and selflessness, so I fell into the pit-of-nothing—meaninglessness, despair, exhaustion, existential crisis and all that. Starving and running became the perfectly ignorant solution—I was distracted from big questions around existence and slowly killing myself, which would get me out of answering them.

This is where the Buddhist teaching on the Middle Way guides our way. Between the project-of-me and the pit-of-nothing is that gorgeous but groundless experience of selflessness—being empty of a separate self but full of everything else. We are certainly here in existence and having an experience—but it is much bigger than the project-of-me. And it requires that bigger mind my teacher pointed to during our first meeting. It takes some courage to let our minds step out of the comfort of our binaries, especially the project-of-me-creation-of-you. However, it reveals a whole other level of potential for human beings. Living from that place is where we're headed next. But, first, with our malleable minds, we can chip away at the false solidity of me-you, we-they to find spaciousness and possibility in every situation.

Experiment

- Consider a viewpoint that has changed over time. Due to income shifts, having children, meeting someone, career experiences, moving, aging, illness, anything, you used to feel one way about an issue and now you feel another way about it. Know that this is true for everyone. We are different people at different times throughout our lives.
- As with poor me and perfect me, notice the special thoughts—the superior/inferior thoughts we repeatedly think about ourselves throughout the day—in the project-of-me. Again, when one arises, tell the mind with a gentle, allowing voice that this is only an impermanent thought. Do this again. Know that everyone is haunted by the personal, demanding internal script of special thoughts.
- Each time you pass by a stranger, notice thoughts of superiority/inferiority arising and instead make a wish that you are both safe, at ease and joyful. Try this with everyone in your social media feed as well.
- When friends or family members talk about their day, listen with beginner's mind as if you are meeting them for the first time.
- When you see someone—familiar or in the news— ranting about someone else, recognize that, just like this person, we have all blamed others for our uncomfortable feelings and dissatisfaction with life. We have sounded off about others in our heads or out loud.

- When you see someone—familiar or in the news—making claims about groups of people, recognize that we have all made assumptions about people based on the way they look, where they are from, how they talk, how they dress, how they vote.
- Consider how if your life had been different, a beloved loved one could be someone you dislike intensely, someone you dislike intensely could be a passing stranger on the street who stirs nothing in you, a passing stranger on the street could be your beloved loved one.
- Consider how people you love have done things that hurt you, people you dislike have done things that helped you, and you have had moments of closeness with total strangers.
- Consider that if you were born in a different place, at a different time, to different parents, with different friends and experiences, you would see all of this differently.

Not Harming Living Beings— Going Beyond Mundane Reality

Despite highlighting my teacher's responses to my questions here, words weren't the point of that meeting. The presence alone of the awakened is fundamentally healing. Because they aren't engaged in the project-of-me-creation-of-you, there's nowhere for our project-of-me-creation-of-you to land. Instead, the bottom drops out, and our stories of self and other dissipate in the space. As our smaller mind impulses dissolve, we are left with the vast wisdom mind. We tune into a channel of selflessness and connection, and it invites a feeling of expansion and relaxation. Because of our project-of-me-creation-of-you habit, we will often project that wisdom onto the teacher. However, they are simply showing us what's available within every being's mind. Of course, due to more practice, study and discipline within this lifetime and prior ones, their mindstream is further downstream; but we're all in the stream. When our minds release conceptual categories and open into the wisdom of selflessness, we feel an arresting absence of separation between self and other. Together, we rest in spacious awareness. It's healing and freeing. Touching into that with my teacher, I realized that cultivating and sharing this mind is the promise of human life. Vows, prostrations, not harming—I'd do it all to be of benefit to the world in this way.

And we can all be of benefit in this way. Right here, right now, we can look for an experience of self and other that is fluid, dynamic and interconnected. The exploration of the middle way of self grows into an exploration of the middle way of self and other. As is the case with the self, the relationship between self and other is not solid, permanent or independent, but nor is it nonexistent. Each meeting of self and other is a confluence of our countless causes and conditions coming together. Further, no two encounters are the same. It is more complex than me and you, we and they. Each time we encounter another—even those others we've encountered a lot—we co-create anew. Out of laziness, we interact on a conceptual level that is laden with stale stories and assumptions. It is limiting and even harming to see each other with such small minds. When we approach each other from the wisdom of selflessness, we set loose the stuck energy of me-you, we-they and experience presence.

In other words, when I stop the project-of-me, I not only free myself but also you. When you stop the project-of-me, you not only free yourself but also me. We free each other from all kinds of expectations that trap self and other. Actually, if I am but a stream of my experiences, then my experience of you in this moment is me. If I am thinking angry and harmful thoughts about you, I experience anger and harm. If I am thinking grateful and loving thoughts about you, I experience gratitude and love. The choice is mine. The borders between us are not so clear. When we ease up on the conceptuality of me-you and we-they, we have a more direct and honest experience of each other. When we integrate like this, we sense being part of the larger whole, awakening to its wisdom. People use the term nondualism for this—we go beyond the delineated categories of project-of-me-creation-of-you into a state of expanded consciousness where we experience being ever-changing expressions of life in play with every ever-changing expression of life.

It's not as woo-woo as it sounds, and it happens more often than we think. It's mostly a matter of relaxing and recognizing it. We've all had moments when we've pulled back the curtain of conceptuality and had an experience of self and other beyond mundane reality. Glimpses of this can arise during flow states when some combination of concentration and delight pulls us into nondualism. I remember my basketball-playing brother talking about beyond-mundane moments when the players, offense and defense, became a synergistic being and the ball flowed magically between them. Most of us try to find it through sex, drugs and rock 'n roll. The urge to merge via sex, the desire to drug ourselves out of thought, the escaping pull of drums and singing and dance— these are vehicles humans have used forever to go beyond the confines of the project-of-me-creation-of-you into an experience of nondualism. We transcend even an intellectual understanding of selflessness to physically and energetically *feel* how everything is everything. Ironically, when we lose the thinky-thinky, life starts to make much more sense.

When I first landed in my lineage, I was confused by how our practices included endless singing. Again, I'd come from American mindfulness, which included a lot of silent meditation and talks. Now I was singing all day at retreat— singing the instructions of visualization practices, singing as a preamble to silent meditation practices. I loved it but felt baffled because was spirituality allowed to be such fun? Ah, Puritan training. I went to church growing up and the singing was the best part, but it was only a smidge of the service compared to the sermons and lessons. I endured the talking for the reward of singing hymns, which felt like hanging out with angels. And I was onto something.

Indeed, singing brought my first conscious visit to nondualism in Montreal's Notre Dame. As a sophomore in high school, I'd traveled there with my school choir for a competition. It was my first time leaving the country, and, though we got there by bus, it felt exotic, what with all the French. One day, we took a tour of the city, ordered croque monsieurs with our fourth period French accents, visited Notre Dame and oh the beauty. Our Jewish choir director had us singing a lot of Latin choral music, including a rare version of *Ave Maria* and oh the beauty. Somehow, that day, we were allowed to assemble before the altar of Notre Dame for a spontaneous performance of *Ave Maria*. I sang first soprano and stood between two senior girls who had much better voices. As soon as we started, it felt like lift off. That space, that song, those girls carrying my voice, the whole choir merging, we were flying. I left my thoughts and self behind. I felt filled to the brim and beyond. Somehow I felt completely present and completely gone. I was all of it, and it was all pure offering. And, quietly, I was nothing but love and in love with everyone and everything. It was angel time. When I returned to mundane mind, I suspected there was more to the story of being alive. It was a hit of the highest order. Later that night, I got super drunk for the first time because the seniors let the sophomores play drinking games with them. That also felt altered, but it was self-conscious and heavy as can be. Without realizing it, I was amassing evidence around what actually frees us.

We know there is a reality other than mundane, dualistic mind. We go exploring through a mishmash of tools, some of them sustainable and others not. Some of them attune us to nondualism, and others just help us space out for a bit. Some of them direct our minds and hearts into love for the entire world, and others ultimately drag us deeper into our own world. Once we discover legitimate practices that clear our confusion and invite us into the wisdom of selflessness, we need only our minds to rest there. We feel more open, alert, fearless, welcoming, available, at ease. We become less interested in our selves and our stories and our specialness, seeing it all as a burden and block. We move into a flow state with life—we *feel* the magic of all of life co-creating each moment. We understand that when we're completely present, I'm completely gone.

Because the mind presents quite a bit of whitewater, we need guides to help us journey downstream safely. It is important to choose teachers, practices and paths wisely. We can look for vetted minds demonstrating a loving, stable, wholesome, generative, enriching, engaged and ethical approach to the world. It should go without saying, but it must be said more and more, that an actual teacher in no way manipulates or violates us emotionally or physically. Sure, the practices can bring up discomfort as we move through spiritual growing pains. But, if the teachers have genuinely dropped their own project-of-me, they won't be looking for anything from us. They won't even be looking for us to be their students. Their interest is only our freedom. We also get real with ourselves around why we even seek such experiences. This kind of work is only fruitful if we are focused on the good of all beings, as opposed to focusing on self-interest, power and the such, which will keep us trapped. The point is not trippy experiences but the openheartedness they engender. In discerning our teachers' and our own motivations, increasing compassion and decreasing self-fascination are good signs.

Experiment

- Recall times in life when you've fallen into a felt experience of nondualism, not only with the planet but also with other people.
- Contemplate how if any human mind can awaken to nondual experiences of self and other, all human minds can do it.
- Next time you're hanging out with someone in silence or conversation, drop the storyline of self and see what you feel in your body.
- Recognize that you're practicing mental states all the time and make choices other than the same station of special thoughts in the project-of-me.
- Set an intention to find teachers who can carefully and ethically show you the potential of your mind.
- Consider that it is safe to feel good in the presence of others.

Selflessness for the Win

After a few weeks of hunkering down into the political drama of we, they and winning, I recognized the relapse into self-pity and its swamp of egoic pride, victim mind, anger and harm. It felt so yucky that I took steps to move on. I said prayers for all of us, especially the specific parties involved in this latest political drama. I said buh-bye to most media. I called representatives and looked into election volunteering. I had healing conversations with a few friends and especially one of my older brothers—giving space to share pain, then going big picture on how we've gotten here and how to be better with our minds, speech and actions. I took good care of my magical female body. I said prayers of gratitude for being a woman in this life and all of the beauty that accompanies it, including clearing karma from violating women in previous lives as well as the current vantage point of seeing patriarchy's problems with privilege. I doubled down on practice to generate more moments of wisdom mind's selflessness, which expresses itself in compassionate speech and action. And, I remade my vow to myself to pursue enlightenment in a female body—in this life and all future lives—because that is the girl power this world really needs.

A couple of months later, I visited my parents for Christmas. As usual, I went to church with them and attended their post-service Bible Study where, that day, one of their friends was leading a discussion on Mary. He asked us, "Who is Mary?" As a contemplation, people shared different names for Mary, and my dad offered Notre Dame. Even with all of that fourth period French, it shamefully hadn't occurred to me before that Notre Dame was Our Lady or Mary. Suddenly, it seemed no accident that I had my first encounter with the feminine wisdom of the fullness of selflessness in Notre Dame singing *Ave Maria.* This is some sloppy theology, but the Buddhist in me started thinking about how we're all Mary. We're all constantly pregnant with Mary's feminine wisdom of selflessness, which births the masculine of compassionate action exemplified by Christ. We love our neighbors as ourselves because we are each other. The divisions are imagined—those thoughts are not truths; they are only conceptual habits with harmful ripple effects. When we touch into the wisdom of selflessness, we actually feel our neighbors as ourselves. Selflessness is palpable and ripe with love.

We can live from this place. Each moment of mind is Mary, pregnant with wisdom and prepared to birth compassion. Time to time, we stumble upon it. We discover practices and teachers that invite us into that space over and over. We learn how to string together more and more of these moments. Next thing you know, we feel increasing kinship with everyone around us. Before, maybe we needed a nudge to get that human connection—we needed the details of someone's story, so we recognized that though the plot lines differed we could relate. Or maybe it was enough to know that everyone has a story—every person we pass in the subway and on the street, everyone we see in the news and on social media is traveling through life's vicissitudes of awful, exasperating, tender, gorgeous. Now, we go beyond story. We release the conceptuality of stories and awaken into the energy of shared humanity. We feel at home with each other, in harmony with each other, and it feels good. We pass each other in the store and it's overwhelming how beautiful everyone is. We climb alongside each other up the mountain and sense our enlivening synergy of journey. We step into an airport only to realize it's Notre Dame, and we're surrounded by sleepy angels buried in phones and dragging rolling bags. And, as we try to hide our tears of love for each blessed one…well, maybe that's winning.

Talk Less, Listen More
Not Lying or Using Divisive or Idle Speech

Let's talk about listening. It's a radical act. If we want to resist and rebel in this world of constant content creation and project-of-me promotion, we can learn how to listen. Really listen. Not the *waiting to talk* thing that we pass off as listening. We're talking about listening that helps us all grow up and out of self-absorption and self-pity. This kind of listening is connected—an act of union that immediately shifts our mental momentum from me to we. It's open—an act of acceptance that allows for whatever is arising without inserting the agenda of *what about me*. It's attentive—an act of attuning to the flashes of interdependent insight emerging in self and other. This kind of listening is a way of holding space for the highest expression of a situation to reveal itself.

At some point in my Naropa MDiv, I realized I was getting a degree in holding space. This term is so pervasive at Naropa that we have a joke: How many Naropa students does it take to change a lightbulb? Thirteen—one to change the lightbulb and twelve to hold the space. With holding space, I'm talking about listening rooted in the wisdom of selflessness such that it is an act of compassion. As discussed in the previous chapter, once we taste a bit of selflessness, we see how we create our problems with the dualistic project-of-me-creation-of-you, and we seek to release self and other from this cycle. This is the birth of compassion. Of course, compassionate action includes a wide range of activity and non-activity, but perhaps most precious is compassionate action that invites more wisdom, which in turn begets more compassion. Wisdom and compassion are often referred to as two wings of a bird—they work together to help us soar to our highest expression of being. As human beings, we are verbal creatures. Words are how we do much of what we do. Holding space creates a cascade of healing self and other such that we all wake up more and more, shaking off the shackles of self-absorption and self-pity, increasing the presence of wisdom and compassion in our world.

As mentioned, at Naropa, I now teach an undergraduate course on Social Innovation and Entrepreneurship, and this year the students and I have subtitled it The Art of Listening. The students often come into the course feeling a little insecure about their contemplative education in the competitive world, especially around business, entrepreneurship, etc. They wonder if the job market gives a flock about their rigorous training in insight, empathy, self-awareness and vulnerability. Where on a resume does one put fearlessly openhearted or comfortable crying in public? I don't have answers on this—though I have fantasies about it. Because I watch these students, trained in wisdom and compassion, hold space for each other in a way that is straight up magic. In seeing them support the evolution of self and other—which is both tender and fierce—I get the privileged position of watching humanity evolve in real time. I remind them that they can pick up spreadsheet skills anytime, but this accelerator of awakening is the value creation our world desperately needs.

Because, listen, here is what humans know for sure—too much thinking about ourselves invites misery, more thinking about others invites joy. Some version of this insight roots every wisdom tradition. But that's only the root. As someone who has had the good fortune of listening to countless people as a teacher, coach and chaplain, here is what I know for sure—everyone wants to help each other. The human heart is awesome in this way. We want to be of benefit to each other. We want to do more than succeed. We want to heal ourselves, each other, the planet.

We dress up our healing in different costumes based on the confluence of our gifts and training and circumstances, but we're all searching for ways to do better by each other. Here's a quick sample of some of the healers crossing my path these days: The biotech founder who wants to help our bodies grow their own replacement parts. The coding genius who wants to help us collaborate as we innovate. The lawyer who wants to help us communicate across ideological divides. The other lawyer who wants to help us hear each other with empathy. And the other lawyer who wants to help us have difficult conversations with kindness. The medical student who wants to help us respect those walking the path of addiction. The writer/actor/director/mother who wants to help artistic moms shine. The artist who wants to help us live from the future. The intellectual who wants to help us educate around crisis. The contractor who wants to help us create peaceful spaces for death. The hospice chaplain who wants to help us open to aliveness. These are the wishing prayers of the people we pass on the street and in the store. People, just like you and me, who show up to coaching or class or life with some idea of what they want to get from the world and quite quickly focus on what they would like to offer. This is the big reveal of the search for the authentic self—when we go deep enough, self-interest, self-identity, self-fascination flame out in the truth of selflessness and our only interest is compassion. We want to find ways to hold humanity to its highest standard.

Uncovering and unleashing our noble abilities and aspirations are a result of listening—listening to our confusion, listening to our clarity, listening to our callings, listening to the pain of ourselves and those around us, and being listened to in a way that holds space for our wisest, most compassionate expression of our particular gifts and training to emerge. Because once we really listen to each other and ourselves, we see that all we really want to do is lift each other up.

Moreover, we find that the best way to do this is to keep

listening and holding space. As we touch into our inherent insight, we recognize the inherent insight in others. We can trust that each one of us is somewhere in the stream of awakening, as we all are collectively. People, situations, communities are all capable of waking up to their highest expression; we simply hold the space for this to happen. We do this by holding space with gentleness, kindness, discipline and wrath as we search for and reflect back self and other's wisdom and compassion over and over again. In this way, we can all be social innovators in that we are supporting humanity's growth in whatever role we happen to play in the moment—from lawyer to neighbor to partner. No need to fix or save or the such. We can simply be there in powerful presence, holding space with high-level listening skills.

In the spirit of cultivating such compassionate action, in this chapter, we'll look at how we talk and how we listen because our talking—external and internal—is what blocks our listening. To do so, we'll look at the ethic of abandoning lying, divisive and idle speech in three ways. First, we'll use the ethic as a path to create a mindful speech practice and consider how a mindful speech movement would perhaps serve our culture more than the current mindful meditation movement. This is like trimming the weeds. Next, we'll explore the ethic as a contemplation on inner speech only to—surprise!—see how this is mindful meditation. This is like pulling the weeds out at the root. Finally, we'll expand on the ethic to create a practice of holding space and healing self and other through listening. This is like giving water and sunshine to our inherent seeds of wisdom, compassion and joy.

Not Lying or Using Divisive or Idle Speech— Shhhhhhhh

Before I committed to my lineage, I dated another one for a few years, and this included going on retreat with them in the Colorado mountains after my first year at Naropa. For my first-ever, big-time retreat, I pregamed by doing a self-created, self-supported cycling tour with my then husband whom I ended up divorcing about a year later before I took up with my lineage. If one is to be mis-married for a year and a half, I could not have chosen a lovelier man—intelligent, kind, unassuming and easily the most physically gifted human being I've ever encountered, all the better to flee NYC and explore Colorado with. He has the kind of body that, without even breaking a sweat, can ride a bicycle from Boulder to Aspen and back, fully loaded with food and camping gear, climbing up and over the Continental Divide six times in twelve days. And I have the kind of mind that can make my less-than body follow suit. I completed that cycling tour thinking there was nothing more difficult I could possibly do until I tried to sit still without talking for two weeks.

It doesn't matter how long we've been doing daily meditation—when it's time to see what's really up with our minds, there is nothing like closing our mouths, turning off the world, taking a seat and taking a look for days on end. Retreat's not the right word for what many refer to as the full catastrophe experience—though all of life has been labeled the same. Of the many things we discover when we sit and stay, perhaps foremost is our compulsion to speak and the mess we often create when doing so. When we first see this ethic on speech, it's easy to think, "Oh I don't do *that much* lying, divisive or idle speech." Upon closer examination, we recognize that most of our talking is lying, divisive or idle speech, and it all creates trouble for self and other.

We can start with letting go of lying, which is destructive and exhausting. First, it's pure project-of-me—we lie to make ourselves look better or someone else look worse, which we're hoping makes us look better. We cause ourselves pain by using our speech to further trap ourselves in *what about me*, and we cause others pain by damaging their reputations through our entrapment in *what about me.* Also, we know that lying is out of alignment with the human heart because when we lie we feel regret if only for a moment. Then we begin the depleting cycle of justifying our lie to ourselves and/or maintaining it to others. We use our precious mental energy to cover our tracks internally and externally. Of the endless beautiful things we could be thinking, we're thinking about this lie. How sad is that? And, while we rationalize that we don't outright lie much or at all, let's note that gossiping or any talking about others is lying because we never know what is going on with anyone deep down. Life is more complicated than "she did that." Our chit-chat about each other is not only corrosive but also a huge waste of our minds.

Next up is releasing divisive speech, which is most of our speech. Divisive speech creates division. In its most obvious form, divisive speech stirs up animosity and hostility between parties. For example, our current political discourse in the media as well as our communities and homes is rampant with divisive speech. How's that working out for us? Seems it not only feels horrible but also creates horrifying results in our frayed social fabric. However, divisive speech sows more than antipathy in that most of our speech is divisive because it serves the project-of-me-creation-of-you. We mostly use speech to create storylines about self and other. Even when we're discussing opinions, ideas, events and the roles people play therein, we're weaving a thread of me/we versus you/they. As discussed, me/we and you/they are not solid, separate or permanent entities. Human beings are complex in our interdependence and selflessness. Me/we and you/they are conceptual activities that we habitually create, manipulate, propagate, lather, rinse, repeat in an attempt to find false ground in self-identity. In so doing, we put a lot of oversimplified and inaccurate narratives into the world—increasing ignorance, dualism and division in our minds, relationships and communities. A friend of a friend went to couples therapy where the therapist made her and her husband have entire conversations using literally only the words "me" and "you" just changing their tone of voice and facial expressions. Imagine it for a moment. It cuts to the chase, no? With divisive speech, blatant and subtle, we fall deeper into the isolation and confusion that leave us lonely, angry, afraid and resentful. Speech is how we perpetuate the painful issues of division and discrimination we discussed last chapter. There are immediate and far-reaching effects of the talking we do all day, every day without much thought.

This brings us to dropping idle speech, which requires the courage to look at why we're talking at any given moment. Just as lying and divisive speech feed the project-of-me, we often talk just to reify ourselves to ourselves. I speak, therefore I am. When we zip our lips in a silent retreat, it is stunning how much we want to talk just to have a moment of reassuring me of me. During my first retreat, as we moved out of silence, we were all on different schedules of talking again. At some point, I approached an older man to pay him a compliment and saw that my speaking completely invaded his still silent space. Immediately, I mentally defended myself to myself—justifying my actions as well-intentioned. Then, I admitted to myself that I was feeling needy, desiring approval, seeking validation of my existence—typical human stuff—and manipulating someone into this project-of-me with sticky niceness. And, wow, haven't I been doing *that* my entire life. The violence of even the slightest project-of-me becomes obvious in the context of silence—pardon me as I open my mouth and ME all over you. I have a friend I often run into on a particular trail. Before launching into conversation, they ask consent with a quick "talk or quiet time?"—respecting that trails are a place of quiet time. This approach might be nice all the time.

Of course, we don't have to talk so much. In fact, more and more, we are isolating ourselves out of actual conversation… and then talking constantly online. Within the internet, lying, divisive and idle speech grow stronger. There's nothing to say here that hasn't been said. People behave differently—often with less dignity—online. Things we would never say face to face seem fine to say via screens or hiding behind them. It's a field day for lying and divisive speech, and social media is idle speech on steroids.

Sharing stuff via screens has become expected, even demanded, for our work and play. A boyfriend of mine once trained with a trainer who wanted him to use a fitness-and-food-tracking app, sharing his activities with other trainees he didn't know. On day one, as he typed "almonds" into the app, we marveled at the oddness. Like you'd eat almonds and then step outside and scream, "ALMONDS!" Why are there strangers filling their minds with even a moment of his almonds? I loved him and did not care about his almonds. This is a drop in the bucket of sludge that we're pouring into our minds all day long. With unreflective internet participation—scrolling through social, tossing posts and comments here and there, clicking article after article, watching what's next—we're digging ourselves deeper into lying, divisive and idle speech by engaging in over-speech both output and input.

Our minds are our tickets into and out of pain for self and other. In cluttering our and others' minds, we diminish our capacity to use the mind for the greater good within and around us. As someone who coaches, teaches and writes about creating space within the mind, I'm faced with an ethical dilemma in a world that asks me to promote via social media, the very medium I help many release for the sake of their sanity, relationships and creativity. For me, trying to hook followers via social media would be like telling people to eat greens while I shove sugar down their throats. If we take this speech ethic seriously, we need to push back. We need mental space and intentionality to observe, contemplate and evolve the workings of the mind in order to grow into the best and highest versions of humanity. It is through our minds that we can heal self, other and the world.

Speech is an extraordinary gift. In Buddhist terms, this is the big boon of the human realm. With human thinking and speaking skills, we can access teachings on truth, wisdom and compassion that lead to our personal and collective freedom. This is not so of our differently intelligent but equally promising animal friends. This speech ethic helps us appreciate this gift and use our power for good. It reveals how our habitual speech and content mostly promote the project-of-me-creation-of-you. And it recasts speech as a vehicle for connection and education to promote healing and growth. Thus, this ethic disrupts our pattern of purposefully or carelessly creating interpersonal and societal division with our speech. How many times have our words caused harm to strangers, our communities, our precious loved ones? When we really think about it, it gives us pause.

And pausing is what we need to do to turn this speech ship around. Currently our culture is very pleased with its mindfulness movement. And, as movements go, mindfulness is a great one. However, we limit the scope and power of mindfulness when we focus solely on meditation. In fact, it can become self-absorbed and self-cherishing—all about what my practice does for me. Perhaps more healing and liberating would be explicitly expanding our mindfulness movement to emphasize a mindful speech practice. This would reorient our minds to examine the effects of our speech, which we use all day, every day. It would help us cut down on our compulsion to talk and choose our words wisely when we do. It would also help us cut down on our incessant content creation that's exhausting, even damaging, our minds and relationships. Most important, it would help us consider our impact on others many times a day. It's quite convenient actually—this ethic and mindfulness of speech provide endless opportunities to think more about others, helping our minds repeatedly tap into that root of joy taught in every wisdom tradition.

Experiment

- Set the intention not to lie or gossip and consider what this means in terms of talking, posting and taking in media.
- Set the intention not to engage in speech that divides and consider what this means in terms of talking, posting and taking in media.
- Set the intention not to engage in idle speech and consider what this means in terms of talking, posting and taking in media.
- Share these intentions—no lying, divisive or idle speech as input or output—with others and perhaps ask for help with accountability.
- Employ the old standby before you speak—Is it kind? Is it true? Is it necessary?
- Use the reminder of WAIT—Why Am I Talking?
- The next time you're in conversations that take a turn for lying, divisive or idle speech say, "Let's not go there." Notice if there isn't some relief on the part of others.
- When you want to talk about hot-button issues, assign viewpoints rather than arguing your own in order to separate the evaluation of ideas from the project-of-me-creation-of-you.
- Play the game of having conversations with your partner (or anyone up for this kind of thing) that only use "me" and "you."
- Think of content like food for the mind.
- Contemplate how you are serving the other party in the conversation with your words. From their perspective, what is useful, necessary, helpful or healing about your side of the conversation?
- Play with spending longer amounts of time in silence with yourself and with others. This can mean not

talking as well as taking in less content. The amount of time is specific to your situation, and you can ask folks around you to help you out. Silence is often a great topic of conversation (!) that can inspire others to try it out as well.

Not Lying or Using Divisive or Idle Speech— Hello, MIND, my Old Friend

In some ways, the super-challenging cycling tour was decent preparation for the mental tour of retreat. People would ask me, "How did you pedal up all of those massive mountain pass roads?" Pedal by pedal. No big secret—step by step is the path to all of our accomplishments. How does one write a book? Word by word. How does one stay sober? Day by day. How does one sustain meditation? Breath by breath. How does one release lying, divisive and idle mental chatter that perpetuates pain, division and ignorance? Thought by thought. When we spend quiet time with our minds, moment by moment, we can watch and feel all of that lying, divisive, idle internal speech settle down to reveal the wide-open space of wisdom and compassion. Of all the zillion step-by-step endeavors in my overachieving existence, nothing has leveled up my experience of being human like the sustained practice of retreat. Consistently and relentlessly holding space for myself cracked the code on what would help me be helpful in this world.

In the previous section, we applied the ethic of abandoning lying, divisive and idle speech to what was coming out of our mouths. Now, we go deeper to consider abandoning lying, divisive and idle speech within our minds for three reasons: 1) This is how we release the project-of-me. 2) This is how we each offer others our wisest, most compassionate mind and speech. 3) We can never hold space for anyone else and contribute to collective healing if we're seduced by our mental chatter. We learn how to hold space for others by holding space for ourselves. When we release lying, divisive and idle speech within our minds, we are holding space for our inherent wisdom and compassion to arise. This is meditation. In our culture, we are developing a narrative of meditation as relaxation. The experience can be relaxing, but meditation is far more radical and subversive than relaxing. Meditation is how we reveal inherent wisdom—the insight into interdependence and selflessness. And we do this by releasing habitual thought, thought by thought.

During meditation, we develop a different relationship to thoughts. Rather than following thoughts, believing thoughts, acting on thoughts, speaking thoughts, we watch thoughts arise, abide, release on their own, like clouds coming and going in the big blue sky of mind. Experiencing the insubstantiality of thoughts as well as the space between and around them gives us great peace. Even if the meditation session is full of stormy thoughts, for the rest of that day and over time, we experience more ease of being because we know and feel how thoughts come and go. We need not follow, believe, act on or speak thoughts.

Moreover, and more to the point, let's note that most of our thoughts are thoughts about ourselves—special thoughts in the project-of-me. These include our stories of vanity and inadequacy, fear and anxiety, pride and prejudice, victory and defeat, shame and blame, self-righteousness and defensiveness, self-criticism versus other-criticism, self-obsession versus other-obsession, so on and so on. Our myriad stories of self are rooted in personal patterns, familial conditioning and cultural socialization. These stories include the superiority and inferiority we've been taught around race, ethnicity, gender, sex, sexuality, body size, ability, age, income, education, etc. All of these stories, even when they seem huge and impenetrable, are simply built thought by thought; so they are released thought by thought. When we meditate and let these thoughts be, we are releasing the lying, divisive and idle mental chatter that perpetuates pain, division and ignorance within and among us. We are releasing the binds of the project-of-me. And, when we do this, we touch the wisdom of selflessness and that feels really good. We may even feel physically full and expansive or spacious and open. We may even feel tremendous pleasure. So, sure, meditation is relaxing because freedom from the project-of-me feels fantastic. Again, that root of joy is thinking less about ourselves.

In being intentional about the liberative potential of meditation, we push back on our cultural narrative that is playing fast and loose with meditation as relaxation and, frankly, dumbing it down. These days, we're calling anything focused or repetitive or chill meditative—like riding a bike uphill or listening to an app to go night-night or smoking weed. Such activities might put us in flow or calm us down or gift a hit of nondualism. But those sporadic states are not designed to ultimately and finally free us from the habitual, conditioned trance of self that divides, degrades and destroys our humanity, moment by moment, year by year, life by life. Indeed, as many have noted, meditation as relaxation can be a sedative that helps us sustain behavior that causes pain for self and other. Keep calm and carry on with the unethical business as usual as we meditate to numb our broken hearts that ache to heal self and other.

This misunderstanding of meditation plays into another unproductive narrative, which is the false dualism of meditation and social action. There's a thought floating around that it's either/or on meditating or protesting, so to speak. Done properly, the two are complementary. If we are truly meditating and releasing the project-of-me, then we're dissolving the division between self and other and growing in the wisdom of interdependence and selflessness. As discussed, this wisdom births compassion such that your pain and your joy are also my pain and my joy—that's the state we're moving toward in meditation. Thus, any injustice and abuse against the so-called other is felt by the self as its own. Social justice is the natural outcome of a mind that is meditating—releasing the lying, divisive, idle internal speech that separates us. Further, as discussed, such a mind understands that the object of protest isn't "those people over there" but the mental states we all experience that perpetuate the ignorance of dividing into me-you and we-they. So that mind of wisdom sees opportunities for protesting ignorant thoughts all the time, within oneself and around oneself. We talked about those two wings of the bird helping us soar to our highest expression as wisdom and compassion, and meditation and social action can be another way to think of those wings. We can engage in meditation and social action all day, every day as we train our minds to act with wisdom and compassion toward self and other.

This brings us to the compassion of holding space for ourselves in meditation. As discussed, compassion contains a mix of approaches and can encompass not only gentleness and kindness but also discipline and wrath. In meditation, our gentleness is our lack of expectations. We cultivate complete acceptance of our experience, including accepting our aversion to acceptance. With kindness, we observe our minds with non-judgment. All human beings have all kinds of thoughts—peaceful and pornographic, gracious and greedy, tender and tyrannical. In meditation, it's all just noted as thought; no editorial needed. With discipline, we actually meditate. We intentionally place our attention in the present moment, say through tracking the sensations of breathing. When we notice our attention has wandered off with thoughts, we have a choice. We can keep wandering, but then we're fantasizing, not meditating. And fantasy is where we live most of our moments, most of our days, most of our lives. Through discipline, we choose to meditate, meaning we choose to live in the present moment, by gently returning to the sensations of breathing, like coming home. With wrath, we work with the project-of-me's sticky special thoughts that need tough love. Wrath invites us into wisdom—the insight into interdependence and selflessness—by asking a few questions of the thought: 1) Is it permanent? No. In examining this thought, we have already moved on to different thoughts. 2) Is it independent? No. This thought is an ephemeral link in an evanescent chain of this leads to that. 3) Is it special? No. Though we've editorialized its content as special, this thought is mental activity like any other thought. This thought will arise, abide, release like all thoughts and everything in life. When my special thoughts of self-pity stick around, wrath reveals that I am grasping them to get off on the drama of the misery. I'm resisting the release of these thoughts because they help me create a story about me—even when those project-of-me stories are painful, we are loath to release them. Wrath keeps us honest. Thought by thought, we let it all dissolve.

Though it may sound intense, holding space for ourselves leads to great friendliness with our minds. We get to know the project-of-me's loop—lying, divisive, idle speech—and it becomes not only less scary but also less interesting. By letting thoughts be, we abandon mental chatter. We feel less compelled to speak it out loud or act on it. Our internal dialogue shifts—gentleness, kindness, discipline and wrath become our process. We develop renunciation—the ability to be with our minds, our lives, our world without needing to hide in fantasies, distractions, intoxicants. We appreciate silence and solitude as opportunities to hold space for ourselves—dropping the pablum of habitual thought and nourishing our minds with wisdom and compassion. Of course, we can do this during daily meditation and occasional retreats, but if only there were ways to hold space throughout the day? Oh, wait, what's up cool boredom! Now we see that cool boredom is a practice of holding space for ourselves—to listen from and for wisdom as an act of compassion.

Meditation gives us tremendous confidence to be with not only ourselves but also others in a warm and open way. Because as we reveal our wisdom and compassion, we know that everyone else possesses this as well. We are not special in this regard. Starting with ourselves, we develop a new understanding of human potential. As we talk to ourselves with greater wisdom and compassion, we do the same with others. We feel those wings of the bird—wisdom and compassion, meditation and social action—and wonder how we can jointly take flight moment by moment. In turning again to that root of joy, we consider not only the mind we are offering to others but also the mind we are seeing in them.

Experiment

- Commit to practicing meditation for 5-15 minutes for 7 days. Consistency and quality are more important than quantity—meaning brief, focused practice each day is better than spacing out for a while a few times a week. Also, stick to the time you set. If you set the timer for 10 minutes and it's miserable, you still stay for 10 minutes. If you set the timer for 10 minutes and it's blissful, you still stop at 10 minutes.
- When you miss a day of your consistent meditation practice, love yourself because inconsistency happens in human lives and then get back to it the next day.
- If 7 days works out, try 14, then 21, then you're rolling.
- Set an intention for the practice to be freeing for you and everyone else. "May this meditation practice be of benefit to me and everyone I encounter today." "May this meditation practice help make life easier for me and everyone around me."
- Make the intention enormously liberative because why not. "May this meditation practice free me and all beings from all suffering."

- Capitalize on cool boredom moments as opportunities to hold space for yourself—treat yourself to a break from yourself by letting thoughts be.
- Notice how gentleness works with your mind—acceptance of your experience.
- Notice how kindness works with your mind—non-judgment of thoughts.
- Notice how discipline works with your mind—come home to the present moment.
- Notice how wrath works with your mind—ask whether thoughts/situations are permanent, independent, special or whether you're just seeing them that way.
- When self-pity sticks around, ask yourself if you are maybe getting off on the drama and misery a bit. Then find a wholesome thing to do with your body and mind—like a bath or a book or time outside or a walk—and let it all be with some gentleness.

Not Lying or Using Divisive or Idle Speech— Expanding the View

My mom refers to retreat as Buddhist summer camp—there are trees, tents, bathhouses, singing and a dining hall. Like any good camp, we also have rules, and one of them is no bad-mouthing anyone in the sangha or spiritual community. This applies all the time, not just during summer camp; but that's when we're sharing bathrooms, so you know. Over dinner, a couple of summers ago, a new friend and I were BFF bonding, which included sharing tears and laughter over the pain and strange of our last relationships. My project-of-me tempts me with humor—there are endless potential jokes, some at the expense of others, not even particularly mean, but, let's be honest, it's all about being funny me. So our healing conversation was sprinkled with some divisive speech. At breakfast, I picked up where we left off—trying to escape my mind by grasping for more fun. She gently said she wanted to cool it because her former partner was tangentially part of the sangha. I noted the same of mine and appreciated her guidance. From there, we naturally reflected on all that we learned from and with those men. Soon we were crying and laughing again but now from gratitude and insight. That morning, my friend held space for me and I did for her. She invited me into it with kindness and a touch of wrath, and we fed it with discipline and gentleness. We let the divisive speech settle down, and we created space for wisdom and compassion to arise. It was a delicious meal.

Once we start holding space for ourselves, we instinctively do this with others. The way water seeks its own level, our minds attune to wisdom and compassion. We realize that the no-bad-mouthing rule within the sangha—our communities—is practice to stop that pattern with all human beings. After all, we're all in community here on spaceship Earth. Moreover, we level up not only how we talk *about* each other but also how we talk *with* each other. From meditation practice, we know the process of compassionately letting chatter—lying, divisive, idle speech—settle to reveal the space for wisdom to emerge. Because we aren't special, we know that this compassionate process of uncovering inherent wisdom holds true for everyone. We simply need to give each other the opportunity to do so. When we hold space, we allow for the awesome to arise within self and other. It may take a moment or year or a lifetime or more, but the wisdom and compassion are there.

As a practice, holding space for others is the same as holding space for ourselves. And, of course, we are still holding space for ourselves while doing so with others—interactions are co-creative. Now our present-moment focus expands from our breath and physical sensations to include the other person, their voice and our symbiotic interaction. Just like meditation, we bear witness to the process of chatter, space, wisdom through our co-creation. With gentleness, we see our and others' chatter—lying, divisive, idle speech—surface in our minds and words. We accept that chatter is part of processing life. We verbally discharge energy in our interactions based on whatever's happened before this moment, year, lifetime. With kindness, we withhold judgment on the chatter and see it for the habitual release that it is—even appreciating its particular display in this particular person, be it funny, fiery, feisty, focused, forlorn. With discipline, we come home to this moment of connection. Rather than escaping into internal or external editorials, we rest in the experience of being here now—our breathing and voice, their breathing and voice, the physical sensation of being together. As we relax into the present moment, we feel spaciousness, ease, curiosity and even affinity no matter the content of the chatter because we can be with all of it. With wrath, we raise the bar on our interaction, inviting wisdom—the insight into interdependence and selflessness—that enables us to see the bigger picture of situations and thus act from a bigger person perspective. I repeatedly witness this flow—discharge energetic chatter, settle into the spacious present moment, welcome the wisdom—as a coach in calls with professionals, a professor in discussions with students and a chaplain in conversation with elders. When we create a container of compassion, wisdom emerges, which begets more compassion and then more wisdom. We take flight.

Notice that defensive thoughts may arise saying, "Hold on, some people are just bad. There's too much ignorance or damage. We cannot find the clarity of wisdom and compassion in that person, relationship, community or place." A friend recently remarked on the horror of a reality show set in prison. "The show was so full of violence, anger and ego," she said, "that it didn't seem possible to see or shine light in that kind of place." I thought about how some of the brightest moments of my life have taken place with those who have been incarcerated—through my good fortune to teach yoga in an alternative to incarceration program and teach meditation to individuals transitioning into stable housing. In those spaces, I have encountered advanced humanity. Whenever I comment to that effect, some of my so-called students will remark that their humanity wasn't so pretty a few years ago. But this is true for all of us. When I was in the prison of eating disorders, my mind was a horror show of violence, anger and ego. Despite complying with standards of prettiness—or perhaps because of that—my humanity was not pretty at all as I cycled through defeated, critical, vicious thoughts about me, you, everyone. This was another reason why I was committing slow suicide via starvation—we act out negativity when we feel trapped by our mental patterns of the same. Eventually, we all will make our way out of our various prisons—mental, emotional, physical. We just need a little time to take the journey—a moment, a year, a lifetime or more. Recently, one of my coaching clients looked back on her concerns from when we first met and said, "That feels like four minds ago." We meet each other at various points on our path to our highest expression. We can help each other out by holding the space and letting those wings of wisdom and compassion unfold.

To do this, we must learn how to hold space for ourselves—see meditation. The reason we think others are horrible and hopeless is because we think this way about ourselves somewhere in there. That's how the project-of-me-creation-of-you works. Rather than look at my stuff, I'll talk about yours. So we don't stand a chance at holding space for others until we develop patience and faith in human potential by holding space for ourselves. Once we are comfortable with our range of thoughts and feelings, we can be comfortable with others' ranges. Once we touch our wisdom and compassion, we can invite the same from others. Moreover, we learn how to let be our project-of-me patterns so that they don't hijack holding space for others. This self-awareness and self-regulation were essential aspects of my Buddhist MDiv training in holding space. Because I need a lot of practice, I've been gifted with a career of holding space as a coach, teacher and chaplain. Through this, I have seen how personal our lives are and how we each know how we need to grow. We simply need a little space and often a compassionate witness to see our wisdom.

The other day, I had a conversation with my person of interest. We ended what wasn't happening between us some time ago, and I took a breather from it all to grieve what felt like a relationship miscarriage. Recently back in touch, he called to talk through some stuff, an intermingling of professional and personal. Silently, I set my intention to hold space for the benefit of all parties involved—not so easy when part of my heart still wanted to be involved. With gentleness, I listened to what was up with him and saw the moment in the conversation when *what about me* arose. Even though the issue had nothing to do with me or us, there was still a window for me to jump in, as there always is. With the kindness of non-judgment, I took in his concerns and watched the project-of-me plot a course of smart and smooth but divisive and manipulative counsel. With discipline, I let my mental chatter be and came home to the present moment—my breath, his voice, the physical sensation of being together through the phone. As things became more spacious in my being, I witnessed his thinking shift. With wrath, I reflected back his wisdom—championing his openness, awareness and possible offerings for the world. I felt my own wisdom and fearlessness expand as well, and he reflected that back to me. With that exchange, something beautiful grew within and from us that was more important than any agenda-filled tie between us. It felt so good, and we actually felt more connected. Freedom and love unfold when we shuck the project-of-me in favor of wisdom and compassion.

Recently, I heard a teacher repeat that age-old bit of insight that the most important person in your life is the one in front of you. We have lovers, partners, friends, children, enemies, famous figures, all kinds of people who dance through our minds each day—but the one who matters most is the one who is right here, right now, whether it is our partner or someone chatting with us in line. Indeed, that person matters even more than we do. Not in a self-denigrating way, but in that way that the root of joy is thinking about others more than ourselves. Taken further, together we give each other the opportunity to co-create an uplifting nondual moment of wisdom and compassion to offer the world. Approaching life from this perspective trains our minds to pull back the camera from the project-of-me-creation-of-you and expand the view to focus on our exchanges. Those wings of wisdom and compassion take flight—we find social action in meditation or holding space because we can advance humanity step by step, thought by thought, word by word. Conversation by conversation, our speech can evolve into a creation of more wisdom and compassion in our world. It's like wisdom and compassion are trying to shine through and looking for possible human channels to display our shared progress. Maybe that's actually our job here—to be agents in the collective awakening of wisdom and compassion. In fact, wisdom itself—the insight into interdependence and selflessness—helps us understand that our entire lives can be dedicated to elevating the situation by becoming further expressions of wisdom and compassion. The surprising thing is how freeing and joyful this is. It is a gorgeous release—mentally, emotionally, physically—to stop campaigning for ourselves through speech and instead work on behalf of all of us. The thing we often don't realize about awakening or realization or enlightenment or whatever we'll call expanding the view is that it *feels* so much better than what we're currently calling living.

Experiment

- Contemplate you of two, five, ten years ago or even a month ago. Recognize the increase in wisdom and compassion in yourself. Know that this is true for everyone.
- Think about meeting you of two, five, ten years ago or even a month ago. Recognize that it would be a different experience to meet you now. Know that this is true for everyone.
- Consider how your lowest moments eventually taught you about your highest expression. Know that this is true of everyone you meet who is displaying low moments of mind—anger, jealousy, greed, pride, ignorance, etc.
- Spend a day talking less and listening more. Consider how listening is relaxing and healing.
- For a day, set the intention that your conversations be of benefit to all beings, especially the person you're talking with.
- For a day, consider that each person you encounter is the most important person in your life.
- Capitalize on cool boredom moments with others— notice what it feels like to be in silence with others. Are there ways to be in warm connection without talking?
- Notice how gentleness works with your conversations— acceptance of what arises.
- Notice how kindness works with your conversations— non-judgment of chatter.
- Notice how discipline works with your conversations— come home to the shared present moment.
- Notice how wrath works with your conversations. Explore solutions and next steps rooted in wisdom— the insight into interdependence and selflessness.

- Watch the flow of conversations from chatter to space to wisdom.
- Notice when the project-of-me wants to campaign for itself in conversations and give it a breather.

Healers Everywhere

One of my favorite enlightenment parables is about an extremely realized being who's been resting in blissful meditation, probably on a cloud, for some endless amount of time, pretty sure that this is it. Until a Buddha taps her on the shoulder and says, "You're not there yet," and points to Earth and all its beings. Point being, we don't become awakened or realized or enlightened alone. We do this not only *with* but also *through* each other. If we want to be a Buddha—a fully awakened being—perhaps the best thing we can do is recognize that everyone else is a Buddha as well. A brilliant way to disrupt the project-of-me-creation-of-you is for me to focus on you and all the ways in which you are displaying your inherent enlightenment right here, right now. In this moment, how many ways can I recognize your wisdom and compassion and their offshoots of generosity, patience, discipline, gentleness, awareness, loving kindness, humility, joy and so on. In this moment, how are you teaching me about wisdom and compassion. Not in that patronizing, trendy "this person is my teacher" move of self-aggrandizement that says, "I'm learning patience from dealing with this fool in front of me." No. We flip that script and recognize that each person we encounter is already a Buddha—they are simply a few moments, years, lifetimes or more from fully revealing it. And, if we can't hear and see their inherent wisdom and compassion, then that's on us. We have that much more work to do in how we look and listen.

In Tantric Buddhism, one of the reasons we honor our teachers and display devotion to them is to train our minds to do this with everyone. In hearing and seeing our teachers' enlightened qualities of wisdom and compassion, we are learning to hear and see everyone's enlightened qualities of wisdom and compassion, including our own. Granted, it's easier with teachers and advanced humans who are further downstream and shine so brightly. But we can train our minds to go beyond superficial displays of everyone's habitual human chatter by holding space for the highest expression of this person and moment to arise, no matter how deeply hidden. When we pull the camera way back from the surface appearance of our interactions, we find ourselves in the actual greatest show on Earth—where there are awakened, realized, enlightened healers everywhere. Here is a Buddha playing the part of an inmate. Here is a Buddha dressed as a stoned college kid in PJs. Here is a Buddha masquerading as a screaming politician. Here is a Buddha looking at me in the mirror. If we don't recognize the wisdom and compassion in self and other, then we give it all more space to breathe. Because we know that underneath the chatter of our roles, costumes and masquerades is a broken, brilliant heart aching to feel and display the connection and love of wisdom and compassion. Hear it, see it, speak to it, hold the space for it to heal us all.

I have always appreciated Buddhism's nontheistic approach because it puts the onus on us. If we want to improve our situation in small and large ways, then we need to engage in sleeves-up practice in this moment. Akin to the person in front of us being the most important person, the moment of right now is the most important moment. The karmic teaching of cause and effect is not about fatalism but freedom. Our thoughts, speech and actions will yield results, sooner or later. What future are we cultivating right now through how we speak and interact with ourselves and each other? Again, being human is a precious gift because we can use our speech and interactions to heal self, other and the world. Why waste a moment on fruitless distractions, when we can make choices that bear the fruit of wisdom and compassion.

Indeed, holding space for wisdom is an offering of radical compassion that heals and uplifts us all. In our culture of confining self-obsession, it is subversively liberating to focus on the enlightened qualities of others. Once we get into the swing of looking and listening for each other's advanced humanity, there's no greater passion than affirming and celebrating it. This is how we improve our situation within and around us. It's a moment-by-moment revelation of our capacity to cultivate wisdom and compassion in our interactions. Our collective awakening is available right now. We are inherently equipped to feel and reveal boundless joy and love. Whether we choose to see it this moment, year, lifetime or more, we are all already free. Look for it. Listen for it. Someone needs to be the butterfly effect, why not you and me?

Be That Person
Not Engaging in Sexual Misconduct

Once, during sex, a boyfriend said to me, "I'm not a dildo, you know." Oops. The thing was he'd been acting like a dildo lately and that was putting it lightly. My trust had been broken a few times, and I was ambivalent about whether to end it or work on it. I didn't really have the energy to do either, especially on a snowy Saturday when I was in my happy place of reading and napping. So when he came at me with a bare-bones request to hook up, my mind did a bit of math: One, no, I sort of hate you right now and not in a sexy let's make up way. Two, I guess I should. Three, why why why after decades of awareness and a room of my own and a freaking degree in women's studies is there still the internalized patriarchal thought to oblige male desire, heightened by the fact that we live together even though I pay for half of this and even though that shouldn't matter. Four, so much is pissing me off right now. Five, I do not feel like dealing with the abyss of my anger. Six, I definitely do not feel like talking about any of this. Seven, I suppose the path of least resistance is to get in, get us both off and get out so I can get back to reading my book. Romantic, non?

So I used my skill set—Scorpio + MBA = efficiency—to take charge of the scene. Not something most men would complain about. But, apparently, he felt his true intimacy needs weren't being addressed in that moment. And, wow, could I truly not have cared less. Because as long as I was putting out faux consensually—like outwardly consensually but inwardly begrudgingly—I was going to get mine and who cares if this particular moment is not particularly what you want, dude. I almost said, "Suck it up," which was sort of perfect because it's a command that suspiciously sounds like it has an origin story of being less than psyched about having sex. Though it would refer to oral sex—and on a man because demeaning sexually connotative phrases are usually about being on the receiving end of a penis since that's where women supposedly are during heterosexual sex and to be a woman (or heteronormatively and narrowly defined like a woman in relation to a penis) is in and of itself degrading, according to the patriarchy—and oral sex was not what was happening between us. So, idiom-wise, I thought "suck it up" was close but no cigar. That made me think about Bill Clinton and how power differentials can preclude consent. And how, in a patriarchy, that power differential could simply be man—like any man, not the president, or your boss, or your boss the president—over woman. Then I tried to recall which feminist it was who said *no heterosexual sex* can ever be consensual in a patriarchy. And that all deepened my abyss of anger. Yet, despite this train of thought—or because of it?! Bill Clinton?!—my body was on the brink of having an orgasm. Therefore, on behalf of the sisterhood, I was going to get the fuck off no matter what. So do as I say and stuff it, dildo.

I offer that snippet of my mind during a few minutes of snowy Saturday sex as a basic and fairly benign example of sexual misconduct. There are a lot of ways to think about sexual misconduct, but, to my mind, this ethic is addressing dehumanization. We've been talking about dehumanization throughout this book. Each time we cloud our minds and actions with self-interest, we forget that others matter as much as we do. We see others as less than ourselves in some way. This dehumanizes not only other but also self. Because when we lose sight of others' humanity, we diminish ours as well. As we've discussed through all of these ethics, we aren't here alone, we're here together. Human life is a precious, fleeting opportunity to release the false, constructed boundary between self and other. This wisdom births us into compassion, the glorious open heart that moves mountains. We can actually live from this inherent, infinite love for every being—starting with one moment of awakening and stringing more of them together. That's our human evolution. All of these ethics practices are guiding us toward that highest expression of humanity. There is no more intimate exchange between human beings than sex; as such, it presents our greatest opening to dehumanize or humanize self and other. In this way, sex can be a portal to awakening. We know this. Beyond any biological urge to reproduce, we yearn for that merging of being. As our most potent opportunity to release the boundary of self and other, sex presents a doorway into essentially heaven or hell or some sloppy state of mind somewhere in between. Perhaps more than any other ethic, exploring sexual misconduct allows us to examine our spectrum of evolution from ignorant self-interest to awakened wisdom and compassion.

We can probably agree that one of the most extreme examples of dehumanization is rape, which is the ultimate form of sexual misconduct. Indeed, rape is so gross a violation of sex that it isn't even an act of sex but an act of violence and power. A person committing rape has ceased to see the other person as a human—with their own needs, agency, life—and instead made them an object upon which to act out rage and confusion. In that soulless state of absolute self-interest and self-pity, there is no other, only self. As a woman, I could have easily pulled an opening example from rape and the neighborhood around it on the spectrum of sexual misconduct—the countless instances of sexual objectification and dehumanization that at least half the world experiences on a regular basis. Instead, as a way to emphasize that we all misuse sex, I chose an opening example where I was self-interested and self-pitying, checked out and numbed out, and thus objectifying and dehumanizing my partner and myself. Mind you, that event was not rape on any side of the equation; it wasn't even in the galaxy of rape. My boyfriend was enjoying his requested p-in-v to which I had consented and was technically enjoying as well, and his dildo remark was a playful suggestion to slow things down for more of a good time. That said, his sarcasm was masking his feeling rejected and longing for more connection, and my distracted, aggressive race to the top was a defense against my sadness about the state of our union. All the feelings between us were on display.

Sex creates this space where all of our desires, emotions and obstacles arise, inviting us to sort through our psychic and physical defenses en route to dissolving the boundary between self and other. In its shocking intimacy with other, sex is perhaps our most revealing mirror of self. Yet, all too often, we hide from that fertile honesty around self and other; instead we spend our sexual energy in a murky, self-absorbed space that might feel momentarily good or not. Somehow, we use sex to separate rather than connect and then wonder why we're not truly satisfied. Deep down, we know we're not fulfilling the potential of sex. Somewhere in our awareness, we're wondering about the other end of the spectrum.

In the spirit of opening the door to sex as a spiritual practice, in this chapter, we'll look at the ethic of not engaging in sexual misconduct in three ways. First, we'll use the ethic as a path to ensure consent within sexual activity. This is like trimming the weeds. Next, we'll explore the ethic as a contemplation on embodiment as a precious journey of awakening. This is like pulling the weeds out at the root. Finally, we'll expand on the ethic to honor the sacred space of sexual spiritual practice. This is like giving water and sunshine to our inherent seeds of wisdom, compassion and joy.

For many of us, our first encounter with any ethics practice is religious-based sexual rules on how to be good boys and girls—namely, keep your hands off each other! This results in a mind that represses and shames sexuality and a culture that limits our understanding, vocabulary and capacity to experience, give and share pleasure, let alone awakening, via sex. It leads to sex being linked with power and dominance and all manner of violation and abuse. Instead, we can consider the extraordinary energetic exchange of sex and how perhaps ethical sexual guidelines are not in place to repress us but to help us work with the energy and potential of our physical bodies as vehicles of awakening. If we want to take on the true power of sex, we can understand it as the ultimate act of self-disruption. We are physically and energetically joining self with other. This power is not something to be taken lightly; thus it warrants contemplation on when, why and how to put our hands on each other. However, rather than shaming sex, we can speak to the gravitas and beauty of this singular act that allows us to wake up together.

Before going further, let's make a plea for anyone pursuing any spiritual path to think long and hard about their use of sex and sexuality. Sexual energy and spiritual energy are essentially the same thing—life force energy. When we start practicing, we start cooking it up and we become more powerful. However, on our way to the brilliance of awakening, we slog through a lot of stuff. Clarity *and* clouds can arise. So we need to get clear about how we are using our spiritual/ sexual power even in seemingly non-sexual interactions. We're seeing a lot of sexual misconduct coming to light in spiritual communities, and none of this is new under the sun...because humans. Indeed, spiritual communities are especially ripe for joy *and* pain as everyone stirs up their life force replete with insight *and* confusion. It gets trickier with teachers who can be quite magnetic because of their bright pilot lights. It should go without saying that teachers should be following, at the very least, the basic ethical precepts of their paths, including not engaging in sexual misconduct. Put another way, spiritual teaching is about magnetizing people to their own inherent brilliance, not drawing them in to play with your penis. Full stop. For all of us, whether we're interested in sex as a spiritual practice or not, there's sexual energy flying around in spirituality, so we need to examine how and why we might be using it. On that note, I read the Dalai Lama said that the prerequisite to engaging in sex as a spiritual practice is being able to fly. So, as we consider spirituality and sex, let's all take a slice of humble pie and get real about where we are on the spectrum of awakening, eh?

Not Engaging in Sexual Misconduct—
Bodies are Same Same but Different

One of God's great gifts to straight women is talking about sex with gay men. Truly, some of my most educational, hilarious, vulnerable and tender life moments have been talking about sex with men—with men who have sex with men. Perhaps some of my partners wouldn't want to hear that some of their favorite pleasures have been brought to them thanks to gay men. The More You Know. So, too, gay men have held space for some of my deepest pain and confusion around sex with men. Recently, one of my beloveds—the gay younger brother I never knew I needed—was telling me about some sexy sex with his pretty partner. He said that, at a certain point, he could tell his partner wasn't super into it; so my friend stopped the whole show. My friend recounted that he and his partner talked afterward about how consent isn't something that only happens at the start of sexual activity but something that needs to be affirmed throughout. He said this all as if it was surely my experience as well. And I had so. many. thoughts.

One of the benefits of meditation is a larger, slower experience of mind such that we can hold space for ourselves, as discussed last chapter. In that space, we watch the churn of thoughts arise, let them settle and then sort for wisdom and compassion. With triggering topics, we see conflicted, contradictory thoughts scrapping it out in confusion. My scrum of thoughts about my beloved friend, his partner and their consent conversation included admiration, curiosity, jealousy and a very loud "kids today and their fucking consent." Wait, don't I have a degree in women's studies? My mind felt like our larger societal cacophony about consent—it's obvious, it's confusing, it's necessary, it kills seduction...what is it even?

The consent conversation seems to be the latest round of the sexual misconduct conversation. We've more openly abandoned "get your hands off each other" because, really, when have humans ever kept their hands off each other. Yet, we still want some guiding principles because, well, rape and the neighborhood around it. Sex involves power and bodies and many opportunities for violation. As always, humans are looking for some middle way between no sex and no-holds-barred sex. Consent has emerged as the term of the hour to grapple with the ethics of sexual activity in a world of varying power dynamics. This contemplation is fruitful for us personally and collectively—not only when it comes to sex but also when it comes to our humanness. Some aspects of this conversation feel boring or triggering or insulting, and some feel sexy or delicious or provocative. That's sex. That's life. Everything is everything.

The feminine principle or wisdom exploration of consent reveals the playing field of our bodies, identities, power and priority. This is a conversation we initially have with ourselves if we're interested in evolving personally and collectively. Recall that wisdom is the insight into our interdependence and emptiness of self. Yet, in our fear of the gorgeous groundlessness of selflessness, we ignorantly create identities of me-you and we-they, sorting us all into conceptual categories that get labeled as superior and inferior. We latch onto these identities and play them out within our minds and lives, furthering power differentials between me-you and we-they. Until we don't.

The wisdom aspect of the consent conversation considers how our bodies are tagged with our identities—gender, sex, sexuality, race, ethnicity, class, size, ability, age, etc. The need for affirmative consent acknowledges that some bodies have more power—physically, socially, politically, economically and historically—and we are bringing these power differentials into sex. Relatedly, we are each walking into sex—and life— with socialized stories of superiority and inferiority about self and other. Which bodies are worth more? Which bodies get more choice? Which bodies are stronger? Which bodies have their pleasure prioritized? Which bodies have their pleasure disregarded? Which bodies are supposed to orgasm for the full sex act? Which bodies are supposedly not required to orgasm for the full sex act? Which bodies do we learn how to pleasure and which bodies do we not learn how to pleasure (our own included)? The wisdom of affirmative consent levels the playing field by asking all parties to give voluntary, informed, explicit, enthusiastic communication regarding what we want to do before and throughout each and every sexual encounter. This means we all hold space to ensure that sexual activity is always understood as humans of equal worth connecting with each other rather than any human abusing another in an act of power or even violence that dehumanizes both.

As my friend described his consent conversation, he saw in my expression that affirmative consent has not always been my experience. Not in the slightest as a good girl of Gen X… and as a woman whose body and identity hold the history and horrors of women before me. Together, we briefly held space to mourn the absence of sexual consent across all humanity and time—truly, there are no words to address the scope and sadness of this reality and its painful ripple effects, which touch every single one of us. On that note, let's state the obvious that the wisdom exploration of power differentials around consent is not at all confined to the blatant patriarchal power imbalance within sex involving men and women. Because of the multitude of varying power dynamics in our world, the need for affirmative consent crosses all sexualities and genders. Exhibit A—my beloved friend had to reassure his partner that it was fine to stop. Two people with two penises. As is often the case with all kinds of penis penetrative sex, the pleasure priority was defaulting to whoever is penetrating. My friend and I had a lighter moment of joking about how there could be an entire genre of sex labeled "waiting for them to finish." So many of us have been on the receiving end of such things that to question consent feels absurd. And yet…it's not. It's not absurd to question all of it, to look at everything we're doing within all genders and sexualities. It's not absurd to move beyond base biological urges into choice and freedom. The wisdom of consent asks us what might be more loving, human and evolved.

Again, this is a conversation that happens initially within ourselves as we hold space to notice our thoughts, see our stories of superiority and inferiority, and learn to let them be rather than act them out. It's consistent, internal work that translates into how we treat ourselves and others. It changes what we say and how we talk about sex with our partners. It changes the way we inhabit our bodies and bring them into motion with other bodies.

Many of us resist conversations about consent and sexual ethics because it means unpacking our sexual experiences. En route to greater agency, pleasure and awakening, we must reckon with our pasts and how they play out in our present. Whether we have been through trauma or whether we have traumatized others, it is scary to step into our stories about sex, power and worth. Do I believe myself and my needs to be superior and how has that played out during sex? Have I dehumanized and disregarded others? Do I believe myself and my needs to be inferior and how has that played out during sex? Have I been dehumanized and disregarded? What is the basis of the roles I've been playing? Why have I been assuming that my needs matter more or less than someone else's? Can I be honest? Can I tend to my sadness around this? Can I grieve what's happened to me or what I've done? Do I need to make amends to myself or others? Can I help us all move forward by no longer playing out superiority and inferiority anywhere, especially my sex life? Remember that the feminine principle isn't pretty—she's ruthless. Wisdom digs up our concepts and creates fertile ground to grow anew. In that fresh space, we birth ourselves into compassionate action. This means we come at sex anew, which can be delicious.

The masculine principle of consent is compassionate sex—taking actions such that sexual experiences are aware, accepting, healing, real and joyful for all parties involved. Since sex is the most intimate thing humans can do, it is like a final exam of human interaction. Thus, to further actualize consent and create a compassionate container for sex, we can apply the previous ethics. Are we intoxicated in any way, including using sex as an intoxicant, or are we all fully present? Are we taking what is not given, or are we exploring our interdependence? Are we harming anyone, or are we cultivating loving respect? Are we using speech manipulatively, or are we speaking honestly and listening deeply? Of course, these ethics wrathfully reveal whether we are violating anyone. Moreover, they frame compassionate sex as an opportunity to practice presence, interdependence, loving respect, honesty and deep listening. Yet, these ethics haven't placed any judgment on the kinds of sex we have or with whom we have it. Actually, when you think about them in the context of sex and consent, these ethics are no-brainers.

Also, in embracing these ethics within sex, we bring communication to the forefront of sexual activity. Consensual and compassionate sex is expressive and open, encouraging enjoyable connection. This raises the question—why are we not emphasizing the mutual exploration of pleasure within the consent conversation? "Do you want to do this?" put another way is "What do you want to do?" In our cultural consent conversation, we seem to bury the lede that talking about our desires makes for deeper connections and is usually pretty hot. And, though consent needs to be clearly expressed in the moment, talking about sex clearly need not be reserved for that moment. Anyone who has been in a long-distance relationship or gone to couples counseling or owned a phone knows that conversations about sex generally help sex and relationships. The compassion of open communication heightens intimacy, clarifies expectations and makes the whole experience more alive.

Talking openly about sex also frees us from a lot of pressure—in binary terms, pressure on the masculine to take action and on the feminine to shut up. One of the damaging aspects of our culture's toxic masculine and feminine is this assumption that men know what to do and women don't. This leads to a culture that ignorantly gives primacy to ideas/actions from the masculine and/or male bodies while disregarding ideas/actions from the feminine and/or female bodies. Regardless of gender and sexuality, this binary and toxic distortion often, and unfortunately, plays out in sex. Clearly, there is suffering, including danger, on the feminine side in that we are taught to disregard and silence our feelings and needs in order to please, even placate, the masculine. Yet, there is also suffering on the masculine side. Once, during a class discussion around gender, one of my Naropa students, a young man, asked the room about asking for consent. This led the men into vulnerable waters as they reflected on the pain and confusion of assumed masculine sexual competence. As one of the men put it with a cheeky grin, "Guys are just expected to know how to do things... like home improvement." The awakened compassionate masculine—energy that is available in all of us—does know what to do and when to do it. However, we gain that skill and confidence not via assumptions but via the feminine wisdom of interdependence—we ask, share, listen and learn so that we co-create mutually beneficial activities of all kinds. Thanks to the incentive of pleasure, sex is a super place for all of us to learn how to have open conversations about how we feel and what we want. No matter what bodies we inhabit, learning to respect everyone's voice around sex is a great way to learn to respect everyone's voice—including our own.

Also, talking about sex slows things down—this builds sexy anticipation *and* awareness. Consensual, compassionate seduction means being honest about our intentions and determining if we're on the same page. If it feels too awkward or too soon to talk about sex, then maybe this situation is not ready for it. Or, if we want different things around sex and intimacy, then maybe it's best not to go there. As mentioned, my former person of interest lives at a distance. During our initial meeting, we spent a few weeks in the same place, with some fairly innocent romance at the end; after, we grew increasingly close via phone for many months, spending hours each week building our connection. As we reached the phase of making plans to see each other, we stumbled into a weekend of multiple, multihour phone conversations that dove deep into sex—things we'd done and liked, things we'd done and not liked, things we wanted to do, things we wanted to want to do but never actually wanted to do, things we wanted to do with each other. We all know those conversations—full of laughter, listening, tears and turn on. Days later, my person of interest made the choice to be physically intimate with someone else. While it wasn't a violation by the letter of the law and the situation was complicated, it was very painful for me. First of all, I felt like a fluffer. More importantly, the resultant discussions revealed that our minds and hearts work differently in this realm. So began the process of understanding and accepting that my person of interest was not my person, which was easier with our never having had sex. Honest, intimate, clarifying conversations help us know what we're heading into—all a part of consensual, compassionate sex.

Yet, the thing about sex is we never know what we're

heading into. We are working through a lot of stuff during this massive energetic exchange. Turn on and turn off, pleasure and pain, dominance and submission, affection and annoyance, connection and distance, defensiveness and tenderness, joy and wrath. It's in the thick of it that our compassion really comes into play. Are we ready for anything to arise? Are we ready to go who knows where with each other? Can we actually be there for each other no matter what goes down? When my fifth-grade teacher gave us the technical instruction on reproductive sexual intercourse, she was met with stoic silence until one brave soul raised his hand and said, "That sounds messy." She then said sex could be messy, and so, many couples shower together afterward; at which point, we erupted in groans of horror. Sex with another—too abstract to react. Showering with another—all too real to imagine. Sex is messy in many ways. Compassionate sex creates a container for whatever arises in that mess of magic. It's part of taking care of ourselves and others and being grown-ups about the whole show.

The feminine principle invokes the wisdom to join bodies beyond the limiting stories of our bodies. The masculine principle invokes the compassion to practice presence, interdependence, loving respect, honesty and deep listening. Mutual, open, sexy, aware consent elevates us out of the insecure feminine and cocksure masculine, no matter what our bodies look like. With wisdom and compassion, we kiss goodbye outdated, ignorant roles and enter the messy mystery of sex as joint travelers on a journey.

Experiment

- Spend a day noticing thoughts around superiority or inferiority, specifically about your body. Notice thoughts of criticism, comparison, arrogance, domination, entitlement. Recognize that these are only thoughts that have been taught and internalized, and you could think other thoughts.

- If you are part of a marginalized group, you have perhaps internalized cultural denigration of your body and appearance. You can leverage the mind's tendency to project inner stuff outward and love up those who look like you as a route to greater self-love. For example, offer a smile and pay silent or spoken compliments to others in your marginalized group for a day, week, month, year. For example, as a woman, I attempt to disrupt internalized misogyny by paying silent compliments to each woman I see/encounter each day. Of course, we can expand this practice to include all humans— marginalized and otherwise. This cultivates respect for all bodies.

- Spend some time getting to know your body's preferences through a self-pleasure practice that emphasizes radical acceptance—i.e., it's cool to feel whatever you feel. There are a lot of resources out there. Find teachers who respect you and help you cherish your body and all its ways.

- For a day, do only what your body wants to do— as long as you are not harming others.

- Consider creating a container of time/space to contemplate past sexual experiences and the absence or presence of consent. Do this with professional help if that feels appropriate.

- Consider if there are any apologies or amends you need to make to self and others around sex. Whether with self or others, you can be honest, set intentions and take actions to rebuild trust. With others, consider if it is appropriate or not to involve the other person in your work—i.e., is it selfish to interrupt their life with your regrets? We can always write a letter we don't send or offer prayers/loving kindness to those we have hurt.

- Take a walk and ask yourself, trees, the sky what it is that you want sex to be in your life—what role do you want sex to play, how do you want it to feel, what might sex be calling forth from you.
- Visualize your version of compassionate, consensual, super sexy sex. Know that it is possible. Expect it.
- Talk about sex more with friends, partners and yourself to develop ease with the topic.
- For a day, notice the ways you talk to different parts of your body and try using a gentle, allowing, loving voice and words. Try for another day.

Not Engaging in Sexual Misconduct— A Body is a Terrible Thing to Waste

One of God's gifts to all of us in pursuit of awakening is a body. Actually, to my Buddhist mind, the human body is not a gift from God but a result of merit—positive spiritual energy—and good karma. Indeed, it is incredibly rare to receive a precious human rebirth—to not only be born human but also have the time, space, safety and privilege to engage in spiritual practice. There are lots of illustrative examples of the rarity of this situation—like it's more difficult than the chances of a blind turtle resurfacing from the bottom of the ocean every hundred years and happening to put its head through a yoke being tossed about in the giant waves on the surface. Impossible! Yet, here we are. Whatever our belief system, we instinctively sense that being an embodied human—even with its pain and suffering—is a huge score. We have talked about how human life can be most precious because we have the ability to receive and understand spiritual teachings. Along the same lines, human life can be most precious because our bodies can be vehicles of awakening.

We know that our bodies affect our minds. We take a

walk or a shower to clear our heads. We feel mentally different after a spin class than after spinning through social media. Many spiritual systems employ a mind-body methodology of leveraging tested, proven physical and energetic practices to change our experience of reality. Body-based practices can be especially freeing as they bypass the skeptical intellect to effect powerful mental and emotional transformation. Without contemplating emptiness or making an effort to be more loving, we witness wisdom and compassion bloom because of what we do with our bodies. When we honor, nurture and work with our physicality and energy, it has results within our minds and then actions. It makes sense then that how we engage sexually profoundly affects our minds and lives. Respecting and exploring our sexual activity and sexual energy is another aspect of not engaging in sexual misconduct.

My doorway into understanding the power of sex was not having sex. This was initially accidental and then increasingly intentional. After a standard run of boyfriends during my teens and twenties, I had a big breakup. It was the trauma breakup where afterward we reflect on who/how we've been dating and even why/how we've been living. There was emotional healing and spiritual exploration, corporate careers to quit and alternative careers to create, and the only thing that made sense in my life was Hatha Yoga. Many of us have been there. I took it and ran with yoga, and this meant some renunciation. Of course, a girl who starves herself under stress is all too ready to renounce! So, at first, I went too far with physical renunciation in what came to be my final act of acting out through starvation. Actually, it was the story of the Buddha's renunciation—the teaching on the Middle Way—that finally guided me out of acting out and into actual practice. The short version of the Buddha's story is that he grows up a sheltered, pampered prince who one day leaves the palace and witnesses life's sufferings such as old age, sickness and death. Determined to find the solution to suffering, he renounces worldly life and falls in with spiritual seeking ascetics. He then realizes that extreme renunciation is as distracting as extreme hedonism. So he cares for his body, stabilizes his mind, sits in meditation and wakes up. As is the point with parables, it's a familiar story to many of us, as we often try to solve one thing by going too far the other way, only to find the answer in a less dramatic middle ground. For many years, my glimmers of insight were hijacked by poor me-perfect me expressions, such as eating disorders, until adult spiritual pursuit superseded adolescent performance pieces of rebellion.

So spiritual practice usually involves some middle way renunciation—aka cool boredom. In order to see what's up with our painful project-of-me patterns, we need to take some space and sort through the situation. Throughout time, people have renounced by retreating from life in various ways, mentally and physically. This can include abstaining from sex for a period of time or a lifetime in the case of monastics. I naturally fell into sexual renunciation as I got deeper into my path. My single girl days in NYC were less Sex and the City and more Sirsasana and the City.* It became clear that clearing out our minds and clearing out our bodies are intertwined. For me, and many, this includes clearing other people out of our bodies and thus our minds.

As things get quieter and simpler in our bodies, minds and lives, we uncover and even delight in the sensitivity of being human. We touched on this with cool boredom. Human beings are very sensitive. We can feel life very deeply. Often our fear of sensitivity—especially the physical sensations associated with emotions—leads us into addictive forms of covering up our experience. We pot, binge, anger, affair, achievement away our emotions. Even within consensual sex, we use sex to take the edge off of life. We use our sexual energy as a way to discharge feelings and entertain ourselves rather than respecting its power as life force energy. This

---

* Sirsasana = Headstand

130

misuse can dilute and diminish such power. When we stop using sex as a drug or distraction, that energy becomes more available and we can feel it more readily. We can feel this life force/sexual energy arise along with our emotions or really anytime. We recognize that it is not something to fear. It is power. It is awareness. It is life.

We may also start to experience more pleasure—and not from sex. We hear a lot about the pain, distraction, frustration of meditation and such practices, but we hear less about how it can all feel really great. One reason for this silence is that it's not kosher to talk about one's practice experiences. Though it can be helpful to know of this potential of the human body. Early on, I heard a meditation instructor quote a big-time Buddhist teacher as having said that the natural state of the human body is free-flowing orgasm. Huh. Usually, as humans, we learn how to feel orgasmic from the most obvious route of our genitals; but that's not the only route. In coupling genitals and pleasure exclusively, we've missed the mark on how the human body is hardwired to feel good. We get so obsessed with the big bang of orgasm that we miss the quieter, subtler, more sustainable levels of that sensation. If we create non-sexual space for our life force/sexual energy, it might show us its potential.

This potential of practice leading to pleasure underscores why teachers of such things must never be self-interested. Teachers must never be seeking anything from seekers— otherwise it's all too easy to tell some vulnerable, curious student that you are the doorway to their bliss. And that would be bogus. Because many people experience such things simply sitting by themselves. Talking to skillful spiritual and meditation teachers is like talking to scientists. They are entirely focused on explaining how to do the practices correctly, making sure students understand the instructions and helping them master the techniques. They will also emphasize that any arising of pleasure isn't the point. This is another reason why we don't hear much about the potential pleasure of practice. We go through a lot of physical phases as we clear the pipes of the energetic body and allow life force to flow. See the earlier comment about the pain, distraction, frustration. Indeed, the route to pleasurable practice and life is having no preference or label for the various sensations arising in the human body at any time. One of my meditation teachers had to have all of his teeth removed and replaced because of a car accident, and he did it without any anesthesia. To him, it was just a lot of sensation. Though the point of practice isn't magic tricks, but clearing the instrument of the body in order to affect the mind.

So, in our various efforts of cool boredom or renunciation, we can also be discerning about how we use sexual activity and sexual energy. Honestly, after four years of fruitful celibacy, I contemplated releasing the dating/partner/sex game for good. I felt unto myself, which is a powerful, subversive, liberating feeling for a woman. Then, during my life coaching training, I did a future-self visualization that revealed I could be in a sacred partnership down the road and oh the beauty. I was both unto myself and in union. So I opened myself up to dating, partnering with people practicing what I was practicing, as if that might make a good fit. Admittedly, my return to relationships has not been smooth sailing, though I suspect it has been karmically burning. One period of rough waters was a relationship in which my vagina staged a protest, seizing up like a sentinel blocking entry to the queen. The physical and emotional pain were both excruciating and led me on an extended healing adventure. The physical issue was resolved by pelvic floor physical therapy—a modality that took inexplicably long to find—which involved a series of sessions where a nice young woman in her proper white lab coat went to extensive, clinical third base on me while we chatted about her upcoming wedding. Despite the multifaceted suffering and irreparable damage to that relationship, I am grateful for that episode gifting me a) tremendous empathy around all manner of chronic and sexual pain and b) a zillion conversations about sex, vaginas and energy. And the gem was a trusted healer telling me this:

> What I'm about to say to you is true for all people. It is especially true for women. And even more so for the more sensitive among us. You should only be having sex with a person if you are willing to be that person. That's how strong the energetic exchange is.

It lands, does it not? Contemplating this insight puts a whole new spin on the ethics around sexual misconduct—namely, the selectivity involved in partner selection. Perhaps in putting guidelines around putting our hands on each other, wisdom traditions are not mandating that we be good little boys and girls but wise ones.

In fact, wisdom helps us understand the gravitas of our sexual partner selection. Since the manifold self is a composite of myriad influences, we want to be conscious about what we're putting into the mix. We think about the content we take into our minds—what we read, listen to, talk about, all of this creates our selves that we share with the world for better or worse. We think about the content we take into our bodies—what we eat, where we go, how we move, all of this creates our selves that we share with the world for better or worse. It makes perfect sense then to consider whom we take in sexually and how this affects our bodies, minds, selves that we share with the world for better or worse.

People often joke that partners start to look and act alike. Some of this is due to developing a symbiotic shtick over time. It's also worth considering how we energetically imprint upon each other through sex. According to that healer and personal experience, this imprinting is even more potent when receiving the sexual act. Returning to sex with increased sensitivity post-celibacy, I have felt very aware of what sexual partners are bringing to my body and mind. I recall one partner where it felt like he used sex to take the edge off as opposed to using sex as an expression of love. And it felt like he'd transferred that edge to me—like he was released from whatever was bugging him and now that edgy energy was deposited in me. Or many of us know that feeling post-breakup when we need to exorcize that person and dynamic from our being. Intuitively and experientially, what that healer said resonates. With what we know of wisdom and the emptiness of self, we can appreciate that lesson on a deeper level. Our sexual partners make up who we are and what we then offer to the world.

The compassion that follows from this wisdom would be discernment about our sexual partners and how they impact who we are for self and other. Is the energy of this person and what we cook up sexually something I want to absorb and grow within my being? How does this person and our sexual expression contribute to the mind and actions I offer to the world? Is this union of benefit to myself and others? This means surveying the scene before jumping in—getting to know each other's minds, motives, priorities, hearts. What are we studying, practicing, trying to become? Beyond even the basic getting-to-know-you phase, we use our sensitivity to gauge an energetic match or not. We're reading ingredient lists and checking sources for the food we take into our bodies. Why wouldn't we do the same thing for the sexual partners we take into our bodies? Not just for ourselves but for others. All of that input becomes our output.

Note that employing wisdom and compassion as ethical guidelines around sexual partners makes no restrictions on the gender, sex, sexuality or number of partners or whether we are with them for a night or a lifetime. It also doesn't mean we turn into Judge Judy about potential partners. Everything is co-creation. You and I may cook up a toxic combination, but you and someone new may create healing. So there's an added awareness and humility to the energy healer's advice—what are *we* offering energetically to our partners? Would they want to become us? We attract what we are, so we can consider how our use of sexual energy is affecting our partners and their actions in the world.

I once heard a meditation teacher say that when we talk in retreat we are giving away our practice. If we really start living this stuff, everything we do becomes practice—an opportunity to grow and evolve into the highest expression of ourselves. This holistic practice of life includes our sexual energy and sexual partners. Often we do yoga, prayers, meditation to wake up and then go a little sleepy in the sexual arena. When we get sloppy in our sexual activity and choices, we're giving away our practice. The body is an extraordinarily sensitive and expressive tool—what we do with our bodies directly affects our minds and then our behavior in the world. So we want to be respectful of and careful with this energy. We want to cherish and nourish our life force/sexual energy. Whether a result of gift or previous effort, we can use this journey of embodiment to make progress with our minds so that we can be of greater benefit to ourselves and others in this life and whatever follows.

Experiment

- Consider actions of physical renunciation, including taking time off from sex if that fits your life. Be intentional about it. Check in with your body and mind. Track changes in sensations and thoughts.
- Read stories of saints and/or monastics, especially women, who have abstained from mundane sex and see what they say about the effects on their minds and behaviors.

- Reflect back on experiences with sexual partners with the perspective of wisdom and see how situations affected your mind, behavior and what you offered to the world.
- Contemplate "you should only be having sex with a person if you are willing to be that person."
- Apply the litmus test of "would I be willing to be that person?" the next time you are considering a sexual partner.
- Consider the question from their perspective— "should they be willing to be me?"
- Track your gut response to prospective sexual partners. Honor it.
- Notice how your relationships affect what you and your partners do in the world. Track whether your interactions lead to greater compassionate activity or greater self-absorption, distraction, anxiety.

Not Engaging in Sexual Misconduct— Getting Down with the Gods

Maybe one of the greatest gifts we can give God is sex? As we expand our sexual ethic from "keep your hands off each other" into making sweet, wise, compassionate love, we transform sex into an unparalleled offering of our highest human expression. To my Buddhist mind, sex is an extraordinary opportunity to release the ignorance of duality through an embodied experience of nonduality. Sex takes us beyond our physical perception of division into a corporeal experience of union. With proper understanding, we transmute our primal impulse to copulate into a spiritual act of co-creating wisdom and compassion. In this way, sex becomes a direct experience of awakening. When we treat sex with such reverence, we touch our divinity here on Earth. We enter the heavenly terrain of the sex spectrum.

As we head into a brief discussion on sex as a spiritual

practice, let's note that this is a tiny view of the terrain. It will be limited for a few reasons: 1) This is a complex, esoteric topic covered in its own right in a zillion texts. 2) I feel trepidation speaking about this topic because I can't fly. 3) According to traditional tantric training, we're not supposed to talk about this in a casual or public way. Let's stay with that final reason for a moment. Spiritual practices of any kind can be incredibly powerful and not always in a good way. When you deal with the real deal of teachers, they lay out a clear curriculum with an order of operations because too much, too soon without the proper foundation and preparation can fry our minds and make things worse. We could head into endless eddies of confusion, the bleak and desolate pit-of-nothing, anger and judgment about paths and practice, manipulative self-interest—rather than being of benefit to self and other, we become a danger to self and other. In our culture of wealth and entitlement, we often flip to the back of the book. We equate the ability to pay for and get access to spiritual practices with the eligibility to learn them. However, being a true student of something as powerful as sexual spiritual practice means approaching such a topic with humility, patience and practice. And one of the spiritual practices to master before heading into sexual spiritual practice would be...ethics!

There's a lot of sacred sexuality talk emerging in contemporary American spirituality. Three cheers for humans wanting to be more conscious and thoughtful about sex. That said, sexual spiritual practice is being taught on its own without a larger context of mind-body training, so we see misuse of sexual activity because folks are not properly prepared for this exploration. Mundane mind hijacks the life force/sexual energy and promotes abusive, self-centered, self-interested activities now with a seductive slant. For example, there's an emphasis on pleasure as the endgame. Or there's an emphasis on many partners as non-attachment. All of this mischaracterizes sacred sexuality as an award tour of get off replete with attachment to entertainment, the next fix and more more more. Any practice can be an antidote or a poison depending on how it's used. In contemporary America, is living for pleasure and cycling through sexual partners the antidote for a mind trained in self-interest and excess, not to mention the impact such a mind has on our world?

Also, sexual spiritual practice doesn't even look like sex as we know it. To go back to the Dalai Lama, in addition to that prerequisite of being able to fly, sex as a spiritual practice does not involve mundane desire or run-of-the-mill orgasm. It's a practice of physically working with the life force/sexual energy that is incredibly precise and complex, and it can require years, lifetimes, eons of mind-body training. Further, people who practiced such things traditionally weren't flying around racking up lays. Generally, they were in long-term partnerships or in years-long retreats together. In addition to the physical practice, this work involves intimacy—the stirring of our psychic stuff with a partner and working through it with wisdom and compassion. Partnerships were based on an energetic matching that would heal and evolve both parties in order for them to benefit humanity. Moreover, true energetic matches for sexual spiritual practice are apparently pretty rare, like maybe one or two in a lifetime if we're lucky.

So, as run-of-the-mill beings looking to evolve our sexual experience, where could we begin? Well, for starters, we can understand sex as a journey beyond mundane reality and what that does with our minds. Many spiritual practices use the body and senses to take us beyond mundane reality. All manner of rituals, singing, music, dancing, breathwork, meditation, yoga and visualizations use our senses to shift our mental states. We lift the veil on our unexamined experience of me-in-here-versus-world-out-there, and we feel a sense of oneness or flow or unity. Arousal is another doorway into such a state of mind. In arousal, we experience a heightened state of presence—our senses are peaked, we are so in the moment that we lose track of time, we drop anxiety and our list of to-dos, we lose the bearings of me and you. Our usual human physical and mental defenses are down, which makes arousal a powerful and vulnerable state of being. As such, it becomes a portal for change—things we learn during sex get deep down into our understanding.

A primary lesson we can learn from sex is this embodied experience of nonduality or wisdom. Embodiment creates our dualistic experience. We feel separate in our separate bodies. Our minds reify this feeling by conceptually creating subject-in-here-versus-object-out-there via me-you and we-they. Mundane reality is a thought project of referencing and labeling everything in relation to our constructed selves. In this way, mundane reality is an experience of ignorance because we fail to see the accurate picture of interdependence, emptiness and nonduality—wisdom. As we study and practice, we get glimpses of wisdom; but some practices take us into the felt experience, and sex holds serious potential for this. With sex, we use embodiment to go beyond embodiment in a direct way—like way more direct than singing together. We join bodies to jointly embody nonduality. With sex, we practice wisdom in the flesh. This affects our minds. We dissolve our selfhoods, emptying two glasses of water into the free-flowing river of experience. We lose our selves in sexual self-disruption. In this playground of wisdom, our minds grok nonduality on a deeper level. We then take this learning out into our lives. Becoming one with our partners can help us become one with everything.

As we know, wisdom births compassion. Informed by our sense of interdependence, emptiness and nonduality, we engage in skillful action to promote mutual respect and evolution. In the context of sex, we can imprint compassionate behavior with our partners that ripples out into our lives. As discussed in the previous sections, we treat our partners as full humans—equal to ourselves—with their own wants and needs. Why wouldn't we treat someone as our equal when we're engaged in an event of nonduality? After all, how we treat our partners is very much how we treat ourselves when joined in a nondual physical experience. And, actually, all of life is a nondual physical experience here on spaceship Earth—how we treat other humans indeed ripples back to ourselves. As we learn to treat other as self during sex, we learn to do this always. We form a habit of compassionate respect for all humans in our circle of interdependence.

Moreover, in order to destroy dehumanizing mental/behavioral patterns and balance the scales of respect, we may need to give extra loving attention to our partners, especially if they have a vagina. I'm going to be binary for a moment and straight up talk about vaginas because throughout time humans have controlled and abused vaginas in order to control and abuse those with vaginas. One groovy aspect of tantric practices—sexual and otherwise—is flipping our conceptual scripts to release our minds from stale, patterned, harmful thinking. One script flip can be placing primacy on the vagina and its pleasure. This is where all of that pleasure talk can serve a powerful purpose. Pleasuring vaginas, our own and others, is a subversive and liberating act for all of us. Indeed, some traditional tantric texts make vaginal pleasure the vital part of sexual spiritual practice. Such skillful action course corrects for the abuse of vaginas and those with vaginas in the mundane world. So, for example, in some heterosexual sex, rather than pleasuring the vagina as a means to a penis's end, vagina good times become the main event. And, of course, we can acknowledge and learn from those of us who have been well versed in the primacy of vagina good times for all time, such as lesbian and gay and bisexual and nonbinary and transgender individuals and lovers. On that note, we can use skillful action and give extra loving attention to anybody whose body has been marginalized in the mundane world.

Compassionate sex dissolves socialized stories about some bodies mattering more than other bodies, and we take this understanding into our lived experience alongside all bodies.

Along those lines, even though pleasure is not the endgame when we're elevating sex to evolve our minds, it plays an essential role as a way to honor our partners. When we step into sex as a spiritual practice, we see our partners in their highest expression. We see past their everyday humanness into their divinity. We see them as the awakened Buddha they are underneath their very human habits. We see them as the expression of God that they are despite their very human missteps. And, because this is a nondual experience, we recognize ourselves as that awakened Buddha or expression of God. Our partners mirror our divinity and we mirror theirs. We can level up sexual role-play from the naughty librarian or smoldering fireman to assign self and other the role of divine. Bear in mind, divine can mean all kinds of things—including naughty and smoldering—but overall it emphasizes that we and our partners are treasures to be treasured. Our partners become the god or buddha or deity in the flesh that we get to cherish, celebrate and enjoy. And we become the same for them. What might that look like? What might that be like? And what might that do to our minds? In the malleable mind of arousal, seeing self and partner as divine, we train ourselves to see all humans as divine. This doesn't mean we need to lick or even like them all. This means we understand on an intuitive level that we are all walking around as secret deities, cloaked in our undercover humanness. In the previous chapters, we've referred to humans as angels and the such. Sex as a spiritual practice helps us practice this refined view of ourselves and others.

We can use every aspect of life to wake up and evolve our minds in order to be of benefit to ourselves and others. Sex is a huge, primal force in our lives. Through sex, we can learn to not only humanize self and other but also deify self and other. From this place, seeing our world as a garden of the gods, what are the actions we would take? What kind of world would we create on a very practical level knowing that we walk among deities? Making love can become a place where we make more love within our minds—a love that instructs us on how to treat all humans with the respect, care and tenderness that we all deserve. And, in that way, maybe sex can be a gift to God and our world.

Experiment

- Bring awareness to journeying beyond mundane reality by noticing what activities involving the senses—including sensual, sexual activities—open you up to a heightened experience of presence. What does that experience feel like? How does it inform the return to mundane reality?

- Bring awareness to your next sexual encounter—with self or other—that this is a journey beyond mundane reality. How could this awareness add reverence for the journey? How could you acknowledge that reverence?

- Bring awareness to your next sexual encounter with other that this is an invitation to awaken your wisdom and compassion. How does that shift your perception of sex?

- If vaginas are part of your sexual world, close the cultural information gap by learning about vulvas and vaginas and how they experience pleasure. Put that knowledge into action with great patience for whatever arises.

- Say a prayer for vaginas throughout space and time and all that they have experienced.

- Say a prayer for anuses throughout space and time and all that they have experienced.

- Try on deity role-play and make love to your partner(s) as if you all were co-creating a world of all things possible.
- Offer up sexual activity—yours and everyone's—to somehow be of benefit to the world.
- Explore the gazillion offerings out there on sacred sexuality and follow your instincts on which ones would safely expand your wisdom and compassion.

Give Mine

In shamanic practice, there is a visualized journey we can take beyond mundane reality where a trusted power animal eats us up, licks our bones clean and physically rebuilds us anew, refreshed and ready to step into the next chapter of our human journey. In Tantric Buddhism, which has retained shamanic flavors, there is a visualization practice where we offer up our bodies, so cherished by ego, to all of the demons we fear. This practice is rooted in wisdom—these so-called demons are only aspects of our minds that plague us. In their wrathful compassion, our demons accept the offering, releasing us from confusion and retooling our minds anew, refreshed and ready to benefit self and other. Of course, such trippy practices are not entered into lightly. We must first create a container through training, prayers and the foundation of wisdom and compassion. Properly executed, there can be a profound sense of freedom from these body-based practices, something indescribable. They hit us in a deeper, more visceral place than intellectually processing our blocks to being openhearted in the world. Without thinking about our stuff, we are delivered from our stuff. We journey to places we fear and find that we are fine. We see that our worries and walls were always a mirage, a trick of the mind. We emerge changed—courageous, expansive and loving.

Sex presents a similar opportunity. With proper training, prayers and the foundation of wisdom and compassion, we create a container to offer our bodies to our partners as a path to freedom. Earlier in this book, we talked about offering—focusing on giving and not just taking in order to be in union with life. However, as embodied humans, it is difficult to maintain offering mind because we are rooted in the physical sense of separation and survival, exacerbated by our mental reification of that apparent situation. We live within dualistic defensiveness, protecting our minds, bodies and lives in a prison of perceived self. Done properly, sex creates an opportunity to drop the confusion of dualism and enter the nondual space beyond our so-called selves. It can be a body-based practice of offering. This can be intense, and we probably wouldn't go there without the incentive of pleasure. However, we can flip the script on that needy greed and use sex as a portal to release self-interest. As a woman with a vagina—who has had to employ an extra layer of vigilance and defense in a world taught to abuse such a body—it is this moment of offering within sex that has always felt like the point. Not the moment of getting mine but the moment of giving it. When mutual wisdom and compassion are present and the divine has arisen within, so that all becomes the offering and the offered to. It is a moment of whole and holy generosity when we abandon self-other and enter the river together. We see that separation was always a mirage, a trick of the mind. There is no me without you. There is no you without me. We have only ever existed together.

This moment of making love teaches us how to make love with our lives. It instructs us on how to move toward that heavenly end of the spectrum. We can give the gift of our cherished lives to each other. We can be our reason for living. We can think, speak and act from our inherent, infinite love for all of us. There is no division. There is nothing to protect or defend. That is all a mirage, a trick of the mind. With joy, we can give ourselves over to each other, to the divine, to all of it. We can emerge anew, refreshed and ready, each moment, each day, each life.

Being the Better Angels of Our Nature

"We're better than this." That's what we heard the president-elect say after the riot at the Capitol on the day the 2020 election was to be certified. Well, sometimes. Sometimes we are better than this and sometimes we are not. We are whatever we are in the moment. When I am seething at men on a trail, I am hate. When I am weeping over humanity in an airport, I am love. Each state of being is what I am in total at that time and what I am offering to the world. It feels as if we are a barrage of thoughts and experiences, but life happens moment by moment. One of my teachers says that life is not a barroom brawl between a bunch of thoughts and you; it's a fair fight of one thought at a time. What I think right now is the whole of me right now. What I think right now, say right now, do right now—that is what I am. I am not better than what I am right now. I am not worse than what I am right now. I am what I am right now.

Moreover, right now, I am contributing to what I will be. We can call it karma. We can call it you reap what you sow. We can call it cause and effect. It is perhaps the most boring of spiritual technologies—truly, no incense and candles—but it is also the most powerful. What we are doing right now lays the path or pattern for what we will be. Moment by moment, we create momentum in certain directions. Thought by thought, word by word, action by action, ethic by ethic, we create the string of moments that moves our lives forward. If we want to be better than this, then we need to disrupt the current momentum, thought by thought, word by word, action by action, ethic by ethic. We have the power to propel ourselves toward whatever state of being we so choose. Ethics practice creates a container for these choices. It helps us see the countless opportunities each day to shift our thoughts, speech and actions toward the promise of the human mind. Realizing and offering our inherent wisdom and compassion isn't magic—it's practice.

We can take up ethics practice the same way we take up anything—one moment at a time. We can look at each of the ethical precepts—presented from this path or another proven path—and see where it feels appealing to start. Then, we can ask ourselves what would be the gentlest way to do that in the next few days? And, how would we remind ourselves each day of our commitment to practice? And, how would we acknowledge having done our practice? Wherever we begin, we can track how intentional shifts of thought and behavior further shift thought and behavior. The boring spiritual technology of cause and effect reaps exciting benefits of awareness and transformation. Moreover, we can see how such self-disruption reveals the wisdom of interdependence and selflessness and thus births compassion. We can pay attention to what awakening looks and feels like in our everyday lives.

Ethics practice is also part and parcel of unpacking privilege, which is increasingly, and rightly, top of mind. One way to think about privilege is culturally holding people to different ethical standards. In a world and culture confused by the dualism of self-other, me-you, us-them, we are allowed different displays of mind, speech and body based on our social location—race, ethnicity, gender, sex, sexual orientation, ability, socioeconomic status, education level, age and so on. Some of us might use intoxicants such as drugs and be seen as having harmless fun, and some of us might be locked up indefinitely for the same. Some of us might take what is not given and be affirmed as getting what we deserve, and some of us might work tirelessly and never receive fair compensation. Some of us might harm other beings to the point of murdering pleading and defenseless individuals without repercussion, and some of us might be murdered without regard. Some of us might lie all the livelong day and be given unlimited trust and power, and some of us might never be believed. Some of us might sexually harass and assault others and go about our lives, and some of us having been harassed and assaulted might never be the same. Knowing that our misdeeds come from our suffering, privilege could be seen as the privilege of projecting our pain onto other people through unethical thought, speech and action. Looking at privilege through the ethics lens, we see more clearly the Faustian bargain of it. Any privilege we have could shield and distract us from fully feeling and addressing the pain of self and thus hamstring our human potential of wisdom and compassion. In bringing awareness and transformation to our intentions and impact, ethics practice can help us clear personal and collective obstacles of privilege. Furthermore, regardless of our social location, we all get lost in the human mind's mirage of dualism and resultant misdeeds. Therefore, as we disrupt any systems in pursuit of social justice, it is vital to do the self-disruption that digs up the ignorance of dualism, the root cause of pain and oppression.

As such, the time is always right for the ethics practice of self-disruption, but it feels particularly right moving forward from this moment. In the bardo of our shared pandemic retreat, we have become more acutely aware of our interdependence—for better or worse. Rarely has it been so obvious that we hurt and heal together. If we want to address a pervasive contagion of suffering, we need look no further than our self-interested, self-pitying mental states and ensuing unethical words and actions. We are constantly affecting and infecting each other, and none of us are immune to self's ignorance, greed, anger, pride, jealousy and so on. We all have painful thoughts that we avoid through intoxicants of various forms, thoughts that tell us to take more than we need or deserve, thoughts that goad us into disregarding and harming others, thoughts that inspire us to lie and gossip, thoughts that ramp up a desire to use or abuse our own and each other's bodies. Those people over there, whom we condemn, are expressing mental states that we too harbor and express to a greater or lesser extent.

Again, understanding our shared predicament of self still means that we hold each other accountable for our misdeeds. Accountability is how we learn, and true compassion builds awareness of how self-other ignorance harms self and other. Ideally, this means structuring accountability to include breaking the spell of self through education and training. Further, it means holding ourselves accountable for anything we think, speak or do with a similar seed to that which we condemn. In fact, our complaining about and condemnation of others can be a mindfulness bell to ask ourselves, "In what ways do I also think, say and do things of that nature? And how might I make some shifts starting now?" There but for the grace of God and daily practice go I.

If we have received any teachings or trainings around mind, we have a significant responsibility. To whom much is given, much is required. If we want our world to be better, we need look no further than ourselves. Our world is nothing more than a reflection of us. The collective human situation is comprised of individuals, and individuals are made up of moments. We have endless invitations every day to be the ethical change. Repeated little shifts lead to big shifts and then a tipping point in the way we create our relationships, families, communities, cultures and governments. The more hands we have on the ethics deck, the faster such change will happen. Again, as a person, community, country and world, becoming better isn't mystical so much as math. It is on each one of us to not let spirituality become yet another performance piece of self, but instead a lived expression dedicated to evolving the entire situation.

In this way, ethics practice and self-disruption can bring

deep meaning to a human life that all too easily feels void of it. In our mission-driven culture, ethics practice is an endeavor that will deliver enduring and beneficial results for not only ourselves but also everyone else. In pursuing personal awakening in such a way that touches every part of our day, we contribute to collective awakening each moment of our lives. Admittedly, a cooperative-minded path does not appear to align with our American individualism—also known as ignorance. However, it is often the most seemingly stuck aspects of mind that provide us pathways to freedom. In the spirit of leveraging the self to disrupt the self, we can harness American individualism to give ourselves an individual assignment of ethics practice on behalf of the interdependent totality. We can take our socialized sense of specialness and take on a special ethical calling for us all. We can turn our habit of thinking it's all about me into personal responsibility for the collective whole. We can use our American work ethic to make ethics practice our life's work.

This time when our interdependence, impermanence and uncertainty are laid bare could be scary or inspiring. We choose the adventure. To disrupt the self is an amazing adventure, taking us to new levels of ease and freedom whenever we so choose. We each have the power to realize our wings of wisdom and compassion—and elevate the entire human situation together. Throughout time, and especially now, we have looked to medicines to heal our bodies, but we know we also need medicines to heal our minds. Ethics practice is strong and steady medicine, available across all aspects of our lives all the time. The results are immediate and long-lasting—they might even be our only hope.

Though please don't take my word for it or anyone's word for it. Try out ethics practice and see what happens. Experiment with what you do and how you are. Pay attention and track results. Notice how you respond to the world and how the world responds to you. Every effort has an effect, and each moment is a fresh start. It is an incredible time to be here. The opportunities to be of benefit are boundless, and you are a precious piece of the puzzle. On behalf of all of us, thank you for all you do and all you are. It is always a beautiful time to be the better angels of our nature—thank goodness it is entirely up to us to reveal them.

Acknowledgments

Thank you to my parents, Ginger and Dan Malachuk, for giving me this precious human rebirth and loving me fully through the twists and turns.

Thank you to my Dharma teachers, especially of my lineage, for giving me the teachings and practices to realize the promise of a precious human rebirth. *In all lifetimes, may I never be separated from the perfectly pure guru, utilizing the glorious Dharma to its utmost.*

Thank you to my lineage sangha for teaching me so much about generosity and devotion and also lining the path with endless laughter.

Thank you to my biological sangha, my older brothers Dan and Mike, for being my biggest fans—the feeling is mutual. Thank you to my sister-in-law Katie and nephew Paul for being lovely and loving and affirming my mantra singing.

Thank you to my Naropa professors, especially Judith Simmer-Brown and Sarah Harding, for encouraging my writing and my sharing my writing.

Thank you to those two editors at those two publishers who talked with me about those two book proposals for over two years. And thank you to Stephanie Tade, the ethically minded and kindhearted agent, who took up the cause with this book for another few years. The book deal wasn't meant to be, but the Dharma sister friendships were. All of you helped light my way.

Thank you, Arielle Guy, dear friend and gifted healer, who saw in the spring of 2017 that it was time to put down those book proposals and write about what I was going through right now—and so the rebirth began with "The Cool Boredom of Being a Grown-Up."

Thank you to the men in these pages for gifting me the mirror of relationship and being understanding about my sharing one-sided snapshots of complex situations.

Thank you to my editing angels: Dan Malachuk for your keen professor eye, protective big brother love and steady presence throughout the ten-month eleventh hour. Shane Boris for your beauty way of holding space. Vanessa Coke Cohen for your balanced way with mind and heart. Joshua Shelton for your wisdom way with words and humans. Alika Middleton, Ang Pabich, Adam Chanzit, Tobin Paap, Colin Cooley, Nell Brown, Rachel Garlin, Michael Wertheim, Cecil Esquivel-Obregón and Maya Ray-Schoenfeld for your generosity and kindness. And, Maya, thank you for bearing witness to the journey.

Thank you to my coaching clients who open and fill my heart.

Thank you, Candace Walworth, for being a caring friend and invaluable mentor and inviting me back to Naropa to teach a little bit.

Thank you, Chuck Lief, my inspiring social innovation co-teacher and cherished friend, for being such a strong supporter of my voice, in our classroom and with this book.

Thank you to my Naropa students for all of the insight, warmth, wrath and laughter we cooked up in those circles. Each one of you is a precious gem of a human.

Thank you to the mountains and mesas of this place and all who live within, seen and unseen—you are my closest companions.

Thank you to the wisdom that speaks to me through writing—spending time with you is the most wonderful wonder.

Thank you, dear reader, for taking this journey with me. May you be safe. May you be at ease. May you be joyful.

May any and all merit generated from the writing of this book be dedicated to the benefit of all sentient beings.

Made in the USA
Coppell, TX
24 March 2023

14682214R00104